—MIND OVER—
MOUNTAINS

Sometimes The Toughest Climbs
Are In Our Minds

Máirtín Óg Mc Donagh

'Live Your Best Life'

Máirtín Óg

BOOKHUB
PUBLISHING

ISBN: 978-1-7399578-5-8

Dedication and Acknowledgements

I would like to dedicate this book to my Mother and all my family and to everyone who has helped me on my journey so far.

Máirtín Óg.

Dear Reader,

Thank you for picking up my book.
If you are looking for a Joycean perfect piece of prose or literary perfection with all the T's crossed and I's dotted you may as well put the book down now….

But if you are looking for hope, direction or a true and honest story, that hopefully may help you on your own journey and you can forgive a Connemara man's phraseology and literary nuances, please read on and enjoy.

Máirtín Óg

Man from Connemara Lyrics -Seán Keane

He spent his youth among the stones
The ocean thundered in his bones
His heart was tempered by its drone
The man from Connemara
He always stood out from the crowd
This noble horse both strong and proud
He liked to speak his thoughts out loud
The man from Connemara

When he was young he took a mind
To leave his native home behind
Meet any challenge he would find
The man from Connemara

He made his way across the sea
And started his own family
He never lost his dignity
The man from Connemara
He spent his youth among the stones
The ocean thundered in his bones
His heart was tempered by its drone
The man from Connemara

He carved his place in foreign lands
And forged a new life with his hands
And by his word he'd always stand
The man from Connemara
His life was written in his songs

His melodies were old and strong
They hit you hard and lingered long
The man from Connemara

He spent his youth among the stones
The ocean thundered in his bones
His heart was tempered by its drone
The man from Connemara

**I have named the Chapters in this book with reference to some of the Lyrics from Seán Keane's song – "The Man from Connemara"

Table of Contents

Chapter 1

I SPENT MY YOUTH AMONG THE STONES

SCENE 1
JUNE 9th, 1969.

"Ón gcré a tháinig tú agus beidh tú i do chré arís" – "Man comes from the earth and so must return to earth" – "ashes to ashes dust to dust".

The Priest threw some holy water from a small bottle into the hole. Then he took a shovel from a pile of newly dug earth and dropped a little soil onto the coffin that had just been lowered into the grave. He said a prayer and gestured to the men lined around the hole. All the men held shovels, dressed in black suits, white shirts and black ties, they began filling in the grave. The earth was a mixture of sand and small stones and soil. The echo of earth and stone falling on the wooden casket below was haunting.

I looked around and most people in my eye line were crying. The sun was shining brightly and I could hear the sound of the waves breaking off the stones at the seashore and onto the small sandy beach close by. Then I heard another very distinctive sound. A prolonged, mournful, high pitched clear sounding expression of grief and pain. A wailing sound. I looked up at my mother's face. She was drowned in tears running down her face, dressed in black - seven months pregnant and inconsolable. She placed her hand on my shoulder. I was eight years of age.

My younger siblings, brother Gabriel, sisters Angela and Ursula were being minded by aunts and family friends at the graveside. The men in the black suits were my uncles. They continued to fill in the grave assisted occasionally by friends and neighbours. In the casket lay my thirty seven year old father.

The tradition in Connemara still to this day is to fill in the grave. Such a symbolic task is not left to strangers. After the immediate family has symbolically buried their loved one, others come forward to take a turn with the shovel. It is considered a real honour as a friend or neighbour to get the opportunity to take part in the ceremony, the sharing of grief and respect for the deceased. I have done it on many occasions in my life. On this particular day in June 1969 as an eight year old I had no understanding of the process. Tradition has it that after you have emptied a shovel onto a loved one's coffin, there is no denying death, which then makes it possible for healing to begin.

"Ón gcré a tháinig tú agus beidh tú i do chré arís" – "man comes from the earth and so must return to earth" – "ashes to ashes dust to dust".

As a very young boy I could sense the gravity and immense hurt and loss of the situation and my mother's heart breaking grief. Dad was taken away and would not return to us. He would not sit at the kitchen table anymore or pick me up in his big strong arms and play with me outside. He was a giant of a man in his short life, over six foot tall, fit and strong as an ox. But he was gone from us. Lowered into an early grave. We were all so young and my youngest brother Ciarán wasn't even yet born. What was going to happen to us all?

Scene 2

An Cheathrú Rua – Carraroe is forty kilometres west of Galway on the west coast of Ireland, it's where I was born and brought up. The Atlantic Ocean crashes against the coastline, shaping and forming the landscape. Wild, harsh, rugged and breathtakingly beautiful.

The coral beach is the most famous landmark in the village. The Coral Strand attracts a lot of tourists to the area every year, a welcome local industry that provided a much-needed income for my mother and our family over the years. We ran a shop and a bed and breakfast in the town.

The Washington Post noted in an article – 'Driving in Connemara is a beautiful thing, but it carries with it, a real danger of crashing into the scenery'. I love that thought, it completely captures my birthplace.

"Wild mountainous country, magnificent in every way"- Oscar Wilde - "Connemara is a savage beauty".

My father was a local man, Máirtín Mc Donagh. Better known in those days as Máirtín Willie – The Son of Willie. My father came from a family of seven, five sons and two daughters. The Willie's were known as a very industrious family around Connemara and further afield. In the early 1950's they were involved in trucks and machinery providing services to the public, running taxi services for people especially headed to Galway, the train stations, the airports and the ferry terminals. I remember my uncle Padraic telling me there were very few cars in Connemara at that time and providing a means for people to travel longer journeys outside of using a bicycle was of great help to the community. Bringing home the turf for households was another big occasion, trucks were commonly used to deliver sand, gravel and blocks, to transport hay, collect seaweed and deliver to seaweed factories. Along with the Galway Hookers, trucks were a staple of life and used in all sorts of ways as they took over from the horse and cart era. With all this business going on the Willie household was a busy place. Next, they expanded into the growing fishing industry, purchasing trawlers and working out of the fishing ports dotted along the west coast.

My mother is Theresa (Tess) O'Shea, ancestry originating from Kerry (Glenbeigh). My mother's dad came to the area as a Garda and married a local woman. When he retired, he re-opened a pub in the middle of the village. The pub had been originally operated by my grandmother's family but was closed for some time. When my grandparents got together, they decided to renew the license and get the place up and running again as a public house and added a shop and fuel pumps. The pub in the center of Carraroe – An Chistín (O'Shea's) is now operated by my cousins, Aodán and Rónan.

Carraroe/An Cheathrú Rua is in the heartland of the Connemara Gaeltacht. Carraroe is a peninsula located between Cuan an Fhír Mhóir (Greatman's Bay) and Cuan Chasla (Casla Bay). It is known for its traditional boats, the Galway Hookers and its very unusual beach, Trá an Dóilín /Coral Strand. A biogenic gravel beach made of coralline algae known as "maerl". There are numerous other sandy beaches dotted around the peninsula. In fact, most roads around the village leading to the sea will bring you to a sandy cove or inlet or a small pier. Originally, people lived by the sea because it was their source of food and income, and small piers were built so they could tie up the boats to land their fish and supplies. The iconic Galway Hooker is unique to the west coast of Ireland. This beautiful craft, sturdy and agile and elegant, has become an accepted icon of the cultural heritage of Connemara. Specially developed to sail in the insidious waters of the rugged Connemara coastline, the internal ballast is normally of local granite carefully selected and placed. The Galway Hookers were used for fishing and also had a very important role in transporting and trading many goods, such as turf, seaweed, livestock, and general supplies all over Connemara, the Claddagh in Galway city and further afield to Kinvara and Ballyvaughan.

The Hookers are distinguished in four classes. The vessels are classified by size and load capacity. Bád Mór, Leathbhád, Gleoiteóg, Púcán. The term "Hooker" is associated with 'hook and line fishing', where long lines of baited hooks were drawn through the water and individual fish were caught when they went for the bait on each hook. This method of fishing, adopted by Galway fishermen identified them as 'hookers' and their boats became known as the Galway Hookers.

In the last 15 years there has been a major revival of and a renewed interest in the Galway Hooker. Older vessels are being repaired and brand new boats are being painstakingly constructed. This has halted the decline and possible extinction of these crafts. The Hookers are now used as leisure crafts and at regattas all over south Connemara, the Aran Islands and at the Cruinniú na mBád (gathering of the boats) in Kinvara. The currach is another type of boat unique to the west coast of Ireland, referred to in Kerry as a naomhóg.

The currach came in two versions in the Carraroe area. The trustworthy wooden currach is a traditional fishing vessel that is still used widely around the locality. The wooden currach is stable on the water and handles very well in rough conditions, while the lighter traditional canvas currach is ideal for rowing and can carry occupants along at great speed.

The canvas currach can be seen at the regattas and festivals all around Connemara during the summer months. It has three fixed seats; the three occupants face the back of the boat and everyone rows. There are two oars per seat which are ten foot long and each one swivels on a steel or wooden pin. Some of the best rowers have great balance and focus, it takes great skill and balance to manouvre a currach and have the ability to row perfectly in sync with other crew members especially in bad weather and rough seas. Competitive rowing practices are an all-body workout – with cardio and strength training. My father and his brothers were very skilled rowers. They took part in many racing festivals and chalked up many wins.

SCENE 3

The strong winds clattered off the Velux window in the attic in my tiny bedroom. Another night with no sleep. Awake, thinking and twisting and staring at the ceiling. My 'washing machine' - (my head, my mind, my heart and stomach) was churning around at a million cycles every minute. It does that regularly these days and especially at night, these long dark cold winter nights that go on forever. Fucking flashbacks of situations and circumstances caused by myself I firmly believed. It was my fault. The weight of it on my chest was suffocating me, pressing down hard on my heart and the pit of my stomach. Jesus. I have to get out of this bed. Go for a walk, get out and try and relieve the pressure. I got dressed, grabbed my jacket and a woolly hat and went outside.

I was living in Indreabhán in my sister Fionnuala and her husband Máirtín's converted garage. It was my home at this stage. My watch read 4.10 am - Tuesday October 21 /2008.I headed straight towards the sea. It was raining heavily accompanied by a fairly strong gale. That sideways rain you get in Connemara driven by a strong wind that gets you from every side. I walked briskly, getting to the shore after ten minutes, my heart rate was high and so was my blood pressure, I could feel it. I was flushed and sweaty. I ventured along the rugged coastline almost losing my footing on a few occasions. The tide was in below me.

I stopped and looked down. All of a sudden I felt a calmness engulf me. A strange sense of serenity. I shuffled slightly forward again and looked at the water below. The big waves had a mystic and overpowering aura as they clattered the coast. I wondered? My thought process was really deep, coming from my hurt, from my 'washing machine'. If I jump now the torture will cease. The relentless cycles of negativity and blame, the continuous cycles of inadequacy, self-criticism, self-blame and embarrassment. I will be at peace I thought.

SCENE 4

My friend Ronnie Greaney called asking me would I become part of his A team as he called them. His A team were his staff, full time, part time and a few extra bodies for special occasions. I will add you to the 5am crew he said. The big event was the Galway Races. High point of the year for many Galwegians and especially for city publicans like Ronnie. He knew he could depend on me and I needed the generous 'mulla' on offer. Galway Race week seven day festival is one of the longest of all race meets that occur in Ireland. Estimated to be worth more than sixty million euro to the local economy with around 250,000 people descending on the city for the world-famous annual event. In 2007 the Irish Times reported that more than 700 helicopters landed over the course of the week, with 289 landings on Ladies Day alone. I organised a few flights that year and previous years for friends and family. Ronnie and myself go back a long way. We have the same sense of humour and there's always great banter and craic. To this day when he calls me anytime from 6am, the first greeting is 'good afternoon'.

The 5am crew cleaned, washed and restocked the bars for the next shift. The Dew Drop Inn and An Tóbar were popular and very busy for the races which meant we were flat out for a few hours and gone out the gap at around 11am and well paid for it. During one of these shifts I was cleaning up directly outside the pubs, picking up glasses and bottles, sweeping up papers and cigarettes before giving the pathway a good wash.

I was down on my hunkers picking up cigarette butts that were stuck in the paving joints. The streets leading from Quay Street up Mainguard Street and onto Shop Street were fairly busy with revellers moving around, coming from fast food restaurants, night clubs parties and so on. I hadn't noticed a man coming up behind me. He was smoking and the worse for wear at this stage. I looked up at him as he greeted me. "Ah Jayzuz," he said "If it isn't Máirtín Óg, is this what you're at now," he said mockingly. I didn't recognise him. He didn't let it go there, "The man who had all the trucks and machinery and look at him now, picking butts off the streets, you've come a long way"!!I stood up and eyeballed him. "Actually, I have come a long way," I said. He smirked and waddled away up town. I will never forget that moment at 6.45am on a Galway Street. It was hugely significant at that time in my life. I had suffered massively with the trauma and loss I had been subjected to. I had struggled to cope with the pain, the sense of despair and hopelessness and the embarrassment. The loss of friends and family, my businesses and my identity as a human being had hit me hard. I had turned a corner though at this stage. I had accepted my situation and I was on my journey to re-establish myself. I had indeed 'come a long way'.

SCENE 5

Pressure and chronic stress come together. I was up to my neck in it. The Centre for Studies in Human Stress (CSHS) is dedicated to improving the physical and mental health of Canadians by increasing individuals knowledge regarding the effects of stress on the brain and body. It defines chronic stress as... "stress resulting from repeated exposure to situations that lead to the release of stress hormones". They caution that "this type of stress can cause wear and tear on your mind and body. Many scientists think that our stress response system was not designed to be constantly activated. This overuse may contribute to the breakdown of many bodily systems". A body system is a collection of parts able to work together to serve a common purpose - growth, reproduction and survival. Stress puts the body and the mind on edge. It floods the body with stress hormones. The heart pounds. Muscles tense up. Breathing quickens and the stomach churns. Chronic stress can lead to high blood pressure and heart disease. It can contribute to asthma, digestive disorders, cancer and other health problems. If you don't find a way to manage it, eventually it can affect your body, causing poor health and even serious medical problems that can last a lifetime. Which became the case for myself later on. I had started to address the daily trauma and emotional distress I was dealing with, through Life Coaching and getting back to exercise and going for walks especially. However, some days were just really hard when the stress was ramped up with meetings, negotiations and difficult problems and individuals to deal with.

I remember one particular such day, I had a few meetings with builders and architects and their respective solicitors, not the type of gatherings where I was being applauded and thanked for being proactive and appreciated for attempting to sort things out. Next up in the early afternoon I was facing my own major bank and a further meeting with a finance company for the machinery business. Why was I still trying to negotiate with all these stake holders on my own? This was a global financial crisis. I was attempting to quench a major forest fire with a garden hose! "Let it go man or it will kill you!" I returned to the apartment where I was living in Indreabhán at 4.30pm on a dark wintery Friday evening. I threw myself in the brown leather recliner chair I had purchased for myself a few months previously. I didn't even turn on the lights. I felt totally drained, my chest and stomach seemed to be tied up in knots and my pulse was racing. I felt nauseated and lethargic. I closed my eyes and slowed down my breathing. Just then the door opened. It was Niamh and Eoin my sister Fionnuala's kids. They had seen my Jeep pull up outside and even though I didn't have the lights on they wanted a chat with their uncle. They were followed shortly after by the older sister Ailbhe. Niamh wanted to tell me about her two boyfriends in playschool and Eoin was asking how he could get muscles like me.

Ailbhe wanted to vent about her mother and father. Oh man, talk about therapeutic, the utter excitement on these kids' faces and the laughter they brought to my life just then and there. They were hanging on my every word on my every response to their questions. They LOVED ME (even though at that time I hated myself). These visits became regular and so important to me and hugely influential in my well-being and recovery. That love I felt from those children during those dark times in my life became a thread of positivity that helped me enormously as I navigated myself back from despair. Ailbhe, Eoín and Niamh hold a very special place in my heart and always will.

SCENE 6

I might have spoken to someone about my experience around a particular situation in my life, or regaled about some adventure or sporting challenge I had successfully overcome and they would often say, "You should write a book". I could see that my stories resonated with others and often helped them deal in a more positive fashion with their own scenario.

My mother often said to me "There's a book in every one, but there's two in you." After qualifying as a Life Coach and as I began to coach clients, I appreciated that writing a book would be a great way of reaching a wider audience, I had ample material after all as I headed into my seventh decade.

When I decided to write this book I really did not have a clue what I was doing or how to go about it. Initially, I put together a draft of about 20,000 words, a feeler of the ingredients for something more perhaps. I put up a request on social media looking for recommendations as to how I might progress further. I received some great feedback and the details of many publishers I should contact. I narrowed it down to four and sent off my draft. Three of the four responded. I was chuffed that publishers were interested in the first place never mind wanting to work with me on the project.

I eventually went with Book Hub Publishing in Athenry Co. Galway. We then set to work and you are about to read the result. What is the book about? What is the message or take away for the reader? The content here gives you a glimpse, a wee insight into parts of my life. I invite you to tag along beside me and experience some parts of my journey. Wherever you find yourself at this particular moment in your own journey I hope you take some positive notes and learnings from my experience.

This is not a moan or a bitch or an attempt at looking for sympathy, nor does it contain any gossip or finger pointing. Mind Over Mountains contains thoughts and feelings that are essentially very private. I strip back the covers and talk about my inner most feelings, my vulnerability and my struggles, my battles with life, my situation and my perspective of what was going on and how I have arrived at where I am today. I address my personal issues and feelings that many of you are experiencing in your everyday lives. I bring private stuff that is not often spoken about into the public arena. The topics that are uncomfortable and make us feel vulnerable and bare. The stuff we don't want people to know. I was not prepared for the massive emotional toll it has taken on me - to write this book. In parts I had to revisit occasions, situations and experiences that I wanted to leave well behind. I opened up old wounds and resurrected painful memories and feelings.

Every single one of us is attempting to get our own minds over our own personal emotional mountains every day. I hope as you accompany me on my journey that it will help you in some way with your own, as I share my highs and lows and how I gradually built my resilience to overcome my adversities.

SCENE 7

Monday morning March 9th, 2020 at 8.40am my phone rang. I was on the road heading to a meeting. "Good morning Máirtín Óg. How was your weekend and what were you up to?" said the familiar voice on the other end. "I did a seventy kilometres cycle on Saturday and I was hiking with a group in the Burren yesterday," was my response. The familiar voice was my friend Declan Sugrue, a Kerryman living in Dublin for many years. We had cycled across America together in 2000. I remember putting my hand on Declan's back on a couple of occasions to help him up some steep gradients during that epic challenge. As he thanked me and marvelled at my strength, I jokingly responded by saying "Someday I may need your services." Almost twenty years later - that day had come, roles were reversed sort of.

Declan continued the conversation. "Máirtín you're in trouble, the tests have shown you have substantial blockages in a couple of your arteries, a considerable build-up of plaque is evident. You are in a fair amount of trouble." Professor Declan Sugrue is a Consultant in the Matter Private Hospital in Dublin and a specialist in Cardiology. I had met up with Prof. Sugrue in October 2019. We were both participating in the Pink Ribbon Charity cycle for breast cancer. Declan and myself got into conversation over a few pints of Guinness after one of the stages. I told him Seán Kelly the famous cyclist and our mutual friend had mentioned to me that I should get a specific test done on my heart and arteries and make sure all was 'good with the pipework' as Kelly put it. He had completed the test himself previously. Declan smiled and said "It's a cardiac CT scan - we are doing it for the last five years or so and it does give early indication of any issues with the heart or coronary artery disease. Have you any issues?" he asked. "None whatsoever, but I'm turning sixty next year and would like to tick the box," I replied. "You look to be in great shape and you're cycling strong as ever, but why don't we do a full MOT on you in the new year, let's call it the 100,000 miles service!"!

When I had undergone the tests on Friday March 6th 2020, one of the nurses enquired was I an athlete as my resting heart rate and stats were so good. Electrodes are connected to a monitor that records the rhythm and electrical activity of your heart. The CT scan or cardiac CT angiography accurately shows the heart and the coronary arteries which supply oxygen and blood to the heart muscle. A special dye is injected into a vein in the arm so the heart and arteries can be seen clearly, this allows high quality images of the heart and arteries. I felt a warm flush sensation and a metallic taste in my mouth and a sensation like I needed to pee. It was not painful and I was able to drive home in the afternoon. I did not in any form or fashion anticipate what was to come. Declan continued "I want to get you back up to the Matter a.s.a.p. and do some more tests, I will perform a coronary angiogram and make a decision based on the findings, bring a bag and be prepared to stay for a few days at least depending on what I have to do". I got off the phone and pulled in to the side of the road, Jesus Christ, I don't believe it! After a few minutes I called my partner, Dolores – Declan had already called her, they knew one another very well.

Dolores being a nurse understood my exact details having had the chat with Prof. Sugrue. I was calm as I said to Dolores "we will have a chat about it when I get home this evening". When I returned home later we began to go through the different scenarios, she was trying to be positive for us. I snapped, threw the toys out of the pram completely! Anger, resentment, dis-appointment and all the emotional stuff. I vomited the whole lot out there in front of Dolores. The only thing I thought would never let me down after all I had been through and dealt with over the years - my strong heart! Was it going to kill me? This went on for about thirty minutes. I had to get it out of my system and then I calmed down and we spoke about tackling this together. Dolores had told a few close friends during the day.

I Spent My Youth Among the Stones

Mike and Vivienne from our hiking group called that evening. I could see the shock and genuine concern and worry in their faces, it was very telling. They found it difficult to comprehend that I could have such potentially serious issues. The very capable and very fit group leader was heading to hospital for a heart related procedure!

Chapter 2

THE OCEAN THUNDERED IN MY BONES

Growing up in the rugged, harsh and beautiful surroundings of Carraroe, South Connemara

The Irish language was always part of my life. I am a very proud gaeilgeoir, a fluent Irish speaker – in many ways it's my first language. If I'm put on the spot to react or answer a question quickly, I will think in Irish before I respond in English, I remember being at a very high-level meeting with one of the major banks in 2007 when I was looking for funding for a particular project (I was looking for a couple of million euros). The meeting was going well until near the end, when I was asked a particular question that I should have had an answer to (but I didn't have one) so I stalled and after what felt like an eternity I replied and said "You must excuse me as I think in Irish before I respond in English" This was greeted with laughter and amazement and it led to other language related queries. I never answered the original question and got the green light for the millions!! Ps I also pray in Irish.

The west coast of Ireland is famous for its epic landscape and rugged terrain. It is splintered by the Atlantic Ocean's tireless persistence as it lashes mercilessly against the coastline. Small islands, peninsulas, ports and small sandy coves and tiny beaches peppered along it. Home to the famous Wild Atlantic Way route, the region and its coastline especially, is blessed with a wealth of Ireland's most popular tourist attractions. Living in this beautiful wildly romantic region is indeed a magical existence, bound by the Atlantic and Lough Corrib, rugged rocky wilderness, patchy fields crisscrossed with crumbling drystone walls, majestic mountains, peat – dark lakes and wind-swept expanses of blanket bog. On a bright sunny day very few places in the world can compete with it.

When the notorious Atlantic weather closes in and wraps everything in a thick, damp sea mist or when gales lash the coastline in a fabulous frenzy it conjures the aura and mystical magic of Connemara. Much like a love story, it can be romantic and beautiful, fulfilling, adorable, attractive, magical, special and awesome all at once. However, the other side of this love affair can be wild, wet, stormy, overcast, unrelenting, dark and lonely at the same time. Growing up in this environment, you become very aware of your surroundings and the constant changes and moods it creates. This teaches you to broaden your deeper acceptance and understanding of your surroundings and the complexities that come with it. I believe this improves your balance as a human being.

My childhood and upbringing were garnered in these settings and surroundings. It was a part of who I was and who I was to become. Speaking my native language, living in Connemara on the rugged coastline, surrounded by granite and boglands and the Atlantic Ocean. Here were my roots, my foundations, my origins and my birthplace.

When I left home in the early morning I was facing into the sun as it rises in the east, when I headed home in the evening, I was facing the sun as it sets in the west. The same applies to the moon. As I travelled along the coast road to Galway City, I regularly witnessed the sea crashing across the road at Spiddal or Furbo in the midst of a violent storm, or the sun setting on Galway Bay as I drove home in the afternoon or early evening. This was life in all its glory. I learned to accept and appreciate it in all its guises. Whatever way you enter Connemara and wherever you end up, the Twelve Bens dominate the skyline. They are one of the main attractions. From the coast road out of Galway and the small Irish speaking towns and villages dotted along the way, An Spideál, Indreabhán, An Cheathrú Rua, Leitir Móir, Rosmuc, Cárna, the Atlantic Ocean, Galway Bay and its sea fishing, stone walls and boglands, all make up the beautiful landscape of South Connemara. Head through North Connemara with its beautiful rivers and rich lakes for salmon and trout fishing. Roundstone, Ballynahinch, Clifden, Letterfrack, Kylemore where you are still skirting the ocean. If the weather comes into play on your travels, whether it gets too hot, too wet, too windy or too cold, you are never far away from a good pub. Most pubs serve great food from spring lamb to fresh fish, seafood chowder and always a good pint of Guinness of course. Many also feature traditional Irish music in the evenings.

While journeying around Connemara you are sure to come across wild mountain ponies. The harsh landscape giving rise to a breed of hardy, strong ponies. They are versatile and obedient with great temperaments. They were used to working on the land where they needed strength and stamina to pull carts with seaweed, turf and rock and for transport. In the 1920's the Connemara Breeders Society was founded in Galway. Their mission was to improve the breed by picking the best mares and stallions for use as foundation stock. Today, Connemara ponies are known all over the world for being spirited, sensible and brave with great quality and substance. There are no big cities in Connemara, it is not a fertile land, you will not see crops growing, only certain types of plants, wild flowers, wild herbs and pinky purple heather and gorse bushes with vibrant yellow flowers. You won't see many cattle, but rush hour while driving along the roads can only mean one thing – sheep, there are sheep everywhere! The most common breed is the Connemara Blackface, said to have been introduced to Ireland by landlords who owned vast estates in the mountains along the west coast. Thousands of Blackface sheep were imported from Scotland through Killary Harbour during the 1850's. They are the only breed with the necessary resilience for the rugged and challenging terrain of Connemara. Their wool is very coarse in texture making it more suited to carpet manufacture. Their mountain habitat and diet produce a very lean, sweet tasting meat with a beautiful flavour. The Connemara hill lamb is a very highly valued meat in Ireland and beyond.

In my youth we went to the bog to cut and harvest turf for fuel. This was very educational, of course, in many ways. From learning how to cut the turf, whether you were left or right-handed with the slane, if you didn't already know from using a spade or a shovel. Footing the turf until dry, getting it out to the roadside by wheelbarrow, donkey, or tractor for collection to be brought home and then put away in the shed or building it up in a reek at the side of the house. These skills however only formed part of your education. Building and lighting a fire to prepare the tea and boiled eggs, finding clear water to drink, keeping yourself from ending up waist high in the bog, managing not to get sunburn or eaten alive by the flies and midgets and learning to find appropriate spots for outdoor toilet facilities where you would not find yourself overlooked by neighbours in the adjoining plot, all this had to be mastered as well. Many made their way to their individual bogs by bicycle. Cycling the ten/fifteen miles to get there to do a hard day's work and cycle home again. It was the first time I had seen the practice of bicycles turned upside down, standing on the handlebars and seat with the wheels facing up. It was near impossible to find a sheltered spot away from the sun to put your bicycle, and a long time in the hot summer sun could be detrimental for the tyres. The solution was turning the bike upside down.

Every now and again you get a gentle breeze on the bog, enough to twist the wheels, therefore the sun is not hitting the tyres in the same spot all day.

Flaherty's Pub (Kitts) in Cásla (or Costello) was always a busy spot because of its location and they had great porter. All traffic heading for Carraroe or the Islands, Bealadangan, Lettermore or Lettermullen passed here and always pulled in for food or refreshments. During peak season and turf harvesting times you would often see five/six trucks pulled in with loads of turf homeward bound for various households. Usually a few households (a meitheál) would join together in a village, hire a truck and transport the turf home for those households during the day. They would call into Flaherty's to wet the throats after the thirsty work of loading the turf. We used to love this scene as youngsters. We got gallons of orange or coke or cidona and tons of Tayto crisps while the men laced into creamy pints of porter regaling tales of who had the best turf, the biggest loads, the quickest to get the turf home and so on.

Years later, as I started my own trucking adventures, I brought home the turf for many homes and customers just like my own father had done in his business. Great skill was required to carry out this work and it was a brilliant learning curve for me. Access roads to the bogs are notoriously dangerous, narrow, and not really built to support weight bearing trucks for long periods. You needed to stay on track and not deviate and keep moving slowly and consistently especially when fully loaded. Mastering the swaying effect of the truck on the soft bog roads was a craft and the heavier and higher loads brought massive challenges. I loved the challenge and getting to reverse the truck into position at the different houses to offload the turf was another obstacle to be overcome, but it helped to hone my skills and made me a very good competent driver at a young age. You always got fed and paid after delivering and moved on to the next house. Bringing home the turf to the various households in the many townlands scattered around the hinterland was always a brilliant experience. It brought a great sense of community and camaraderie as all neighbouring households helped each other and took great pride in the operation.

Connemara people are welcoming, hardworking, honest people. You are always greeted with a warm welcome and a helping hand if required. I loved this time of year, late spring to end of September. The weather always seemed great with sunshine and many hours of daylight. I would often hop into a truck at 5am and head away wearing nothing but a t-shirt and shorts, not returning until 10pm.I had my favourite areas of course that did not have anything to do with geography and everything to do with the fun gentile characters that lived there. Many of these men had little or no education but had a brilliant turn of phrase and a library of jokes and yarns in their arsenal. They were great company for the day or the few days I spent in the area. My character as a young man was also developing. I had a great sense of humour and devilment and always identified with my fun side. These characters were enlightening, and we brought out the best in each other. The work was hard and the days long. Gathered around a reek of turf on the bog with a small meitheál to load up a truck by hand is tedious. Add in a summers' morning or evening with no breeze and a million midgets and the job can easily become torturous! Another time-honoured tradition along Ireland's west coast is the practice of seaweed collection. For many decades nutrient rich Irish seaweed has helped sustain the people of Connemara especially. Seaweeds were used in local remedies, diets and farming practices. In the 18th century seaweed was used in glass manufacturing and as a source of iodine. As the decades went by, seaweed products became known as a reliable value-added source to boost the quality of animal feed, nutritional products and soil conditioners. It is also used as a gelling agent in everything from ice cream to the "heads" on beer to textile printing. Seaweed has become a superfood and source of a multibillion-euro global industry.

There are 600 seaweeds growing on the 7,800kms of Irish coastline. Local harvesters cut and collected the seaweed along the shorelines and entered into partnerships with local factories where it was processed and dried for domestic and export uses. The longest standing seaweed processing company is "Arramara Teoranta" (Sea Products Ltd) who established their centralised offices and factory in Cill Chiaráin, Connemara with facilities in Newport Co. Mayo and at Dungloe, Co. Donegal. This work became very important and lucrative for the harvesters in the communities especially in the winter months to supplement their incomes. Another pivotal part of this industry was transporting the seaweed to the factories. Our family had been a part of this process for many years loading and collecting the "weed" for the harvesters all around South Connemara and delivering to the factories. When I started my own business in 1983, I worked with some harvesters to transport their seaweed away in big loads as required. The cutter or supplier was paid a certain rate as was the transport operator. We were paid per ton and regularly delivered twenty ton loads to the factory.

I decided very early in my "business career" that even though I very much enjoyed working with the local customers and community bringing home the turf and hauling the seaweed, this was very seasonal and would not sustain any real growth. So, I decided to diversify. I put plans in place to grow my business and expand into more lucrative areas. I went on a mission to determine where and in what areas I could position myself to help grow, sustain and develop. The Irish economy in the early eighties was in prolonged recession with high unemployment and emigration. The country experienced record levels of financial difficulties. In Galway, Government tax incentives helped in the development of shops, offices and overhead accommodation in the city centre and on lands previously used for Dockland activities. Some social homes were also being constructed on sites around the city. I began to target the construction industry. I had purchased a truck (a Hino tipper) for sixteen thousand pounds. I managed to secure a loan from Allied Irish Bank (AIB). The manager at the time was Gerry O Brien, my mother was dealing with AIB for many years and had a good relationship with them and with Gerry in particular. He sanctioned a loan for ten thousand pounds and my first truck was purchased. I worked in Galway quarries and on building sites around the city during the day and brought loads home in the evening to my own customers and local builders. To complement the truck, I needed to purchase a digger or excavator. I could load and take away material from sites and carry out landscaping jobs.

I located a very good used excavator in Galway – (Poclain 60). The owner had immigrated to London, however. I contacted him and agreed a price and planned to go and seal the deal. My uncle Colm joined me on the trip. He was highly knowledgeable on machinery and had agreed to drive the digger for me if we could complete the purchase. At the height of the troubles in Northern Ireland we headed for London. Two Irish speakers fully laden with bundles of cash! We may as well have been closing a gun deal if we got caught. We spread the price of the digger (fourteen thousand pounds) between us just in case. Stuck in socks and inside pockets in jackets and stuffed inside spare (clean) underwear in our bags. After completing the deal and returning safely from London without a hitch, I felt like I was making progress. The truck had generated enough money to purchase the digger, which meant I just had the original truck loan, which was rapidly reducing, and I now had two items of plant to go to work.

O'Malley Construction was founded by three brothers in 1971 in Galway. They had a reputation for delivering high quality homes and projects with attention to detail both in house design and throughout the landscaped scheme layouts. They were becoming a growing force and had a great reputation for paying their sub-contractors fully and on time. I got a big break. One of their site agents at the time Jarlath Joyce asked me to do some site works for them. I had now added more trucks and excavators to the fleet. Jarlath and O'Malley Construction demanded honesty, loyalty, organisation, dependability and a good solid work ethic as well as good machinery. I ticked all the boxes! In the following years we (my plant and machinery company) went on to become one of their main sub-contractors, as we built up a very solid relationship, working on some of the biggest and most iconic projects around Galway City housing estates at Barna, Knocknacarra, Salthill, Headford Rd. and Roscam and notable projects like The Eyre Square Centre, The Galway Bay Hotel, Jury's Hotel, The Docklands Developments, Fairgreen House and many more.

We had some powerful years, provided a lot of employment, moved huge amounts of muck and broke out a shit load of rock. O'MC and its staff were a dream to work alongside. The truck and plant hire business was turning over millions at this stage. Locally, we had expanded into quarries supplying stone to the Council for road projects and doing site works and foundations for builders and one-off houses. We had a very loyal honest workforce during those years who contributed hugely to our success. Our mantra was good modern plant and machinery, honest diligent efficient workers and a great team spirit. Get in do a great job quickly and competently, get out and get paid. My first truck had cost sixteen thousand pounds and my first excavator fourteen thousand. I had quickly within four years begun to purchase new trucks and machinery. My ethos was that it was better to have modern fresh plant and equipment on finance ready to go to work and capable of producing on demand, rather than old, dated machinery constantly broken down and costing a lot in repairs and downtime. The other positive side was that it created a great brand, image and awareness for the company. This is very important for any business. The public associated us with being slick and very capable with top class machinery and employees. In 1998 we purchased a new excavator at a cost of eighty-nine thousand pounds along with an attachment, a rock breaker for an additional twenty thousand. This new Hitachi excavator weighed twenty tons and the Krupp rock breaker a further one and a half tons. This combination was one of the first of its kind in Connemara at the time. A new Hino truck was also added in 1989, at a cost of forty-eight thousand pounds. My expansion coincided with O' Malley

Construction signing a contract for the biggest urban renewal project of its kind outside of Dublin, The Eyre Square Centre Development. The project was to consist of forty-three shops, thirty-seven houses and parking for four hundred and fifty cars. It also entailed the preservation and opening up of a large section of the medieval city wall, which was previously landlocked in a sea of derelict buildings. This project was MEGA in every sense. Every plant hire and excavation contractor in the country wanted to get involved.

I dreamed, pondered, considered, deliberated, wished, contemplated, debated, ruminated, analysed and speculated. I discussed it with Jarlath Joyce the contracts manager with OMC, he told me to put my hat in the ring/my best foot forward, "What have you got to lose," he said. I set up a meeting with Michael Mooney a company director with O'MC in his office. I made my pitch to Michael to be appointed as the main contractor for the excavation and removal of material, the demolition and the rock breaking for the entire project, and I sat back in my chair. Michael cut a commanding figure as a big man with a no-nonsense straight-talking approach. He calmly asked a few questions. Why should I be considered for the contract? Had I the expertise and the machinery to perform at the required level? Could I be trusted to step up to the mark? I answered each question confidently and with conviction. I finished by saying if O'MC put faith in me by awarding me the contract I would not be found wanting.

Three days later I got a call from Michael, "Start to prepare," he said, "We are kicking off the site works in four weeks' time, and we want you on site ready to go". This was the equivalent of bringing your team to the Mount Everest of your industry. I discussed the truck and machinery requirements with Jarlath and the specifics of rates, working hours, safety measures, insurances, payment schedules and so on. I went into systematic meticulous planning mode. The same as preparing for an expedition, every detail had to be well- considered, thought through, designed and structured. I purchased two more excavators, a 30-ton Hitachi for bulk excavation and fast loading and a smaller 12-ton digger for assisting the archaeology work around the old medieval Galway wall. I added another new Hino tipper truck, carefully increased the workforce, located disposal locations for material as close to the project as possible for shorter turnaround times. In early May 1989 we kicked off on site for the Eyre Square Centre Development site works. We (my plant and machinery business) were busy in other areas as well. The quarry at home was proving very successful, supplying Galway County Council for road works, completing site works for builders and one-off houses. I was operating at full tilt, organising, monitoring, and trying to keep on top of it all was draining, but the rewards were substantial. Turnover had increased from circa 300,000 pounds per annum to over two million and was still growing. Like developing and expanding any business it required massive amounts of planning and energy. It was not plain sailing of course, apart from occupational difficulties with day-to-day operations we started to come up against resistance from other business owners and some of our competitors. In the quarries arena we came to the attention of the 'quarry mafia'. We were winning contracts for road jobs and major projects requiring stone. Influence was used to try and dissuade me from taking on certain jobs, financial institutions were contacted to make it difficult to get finance, politicians and councilors were lobbied. Plant and machinery contractors especially in the Galway area resorted to dirty tactics. Trying to slow down our progress on jobs and even becoming confrontational at times. One theme always came to light. I had experienced it in my early sporting life. It had to do with geographical location and first language. Because I was born in Connemara and spoke Irish as my first language. "Who do you think you are coming from the bog and speaking that fucking Irish". This label in some people's eyes did not entitle anyone who came from this background to compete at a higher level at work or in sport or to try to progress themselves in any way. My method of dealing with this behaviour from others towards me was to become more determined, more focused, more proud, more intent and dedicated to the task in hand. It said much more about the small mindedness of those people than it did about me. In my younger days and especially when I made it on to the Galway County teams as a young footballer it caused self- doubt, stress and uncertainty for me. I did not have the strong supportive influence of my father, and this rocked my confidence and self-esteem when performing at the highest level. Having gained some valuable life experience over the years, I learned not to allow myself to step back or to step away or step down. I prepared better-trained harder focused on improving all the time. In business I believed in myself and my methods 100%. I looked at my wins and my successes, I had been selected to represent my club and my county at the pinnacle, my company was being selected to tackle all kinds of projects big and small, we had very loyal and dedicated employees, we produced excellent results and our customer base was solid. In my younger days as a sportsman, a businessman and entrepreneur there was a stigma attached to me and others who were born and raised in Gaeltacht areas (Irish speaking locations). People were inclined to look down their noses at you for this reason. Getting on to a GAA county panel at that time was a feat in itself, never mind making it on to a team. The Connemara area did not have a strong tradition of football or hurling clubs or any other sports for that matter. The set up in school sports was the same. Students with a desire to achieve in the sporting arena went to football, hurling and rugby strongholds like St. Jarlath's College in Tuam, St. Mary's or St. Enda's in Galway City or Garbally College in Ballinasloe. Parents had to be able to afford the fees for boarders (living in the college) or day students living close by. From a business perspective I found the same mentality existed with many people. Why should a person who comes from Connemara and speaks 'that Irish language' be successful or trying to improve themselves in any way. Stay back there in your own patch, in the bog and the granite on the edge of the ocean. Somewhat like the indigenous peoples of the Americas and Australia and New Zealand.

I detested this attitude and often used it as a tool to inspire me to push on and succeed against the odds. How times have changed in the last twenty years especially. Irish is of course the official language of Ireland. History tells us that it was the majority language in Ireland up through the nineteenth century. The great Irish Potato Famine –'An Górta Mór' lasted seven years (1845 to 1852), the potato crop, on which one third of the Irish population depended entirely for sustenance, failed utterly. Succumbing to a disease commonly known as "potato blight". Around one million people died during this time, most of them Irish speakers. Another million emigrated, reducing the total population of Ireland by about twenty five percent. Many of those who were left were forced off the land by eviction. Some relocated to the cities, where English was essential. For the first time in its history, Irish was a minority language in its own country. The 'Gaeltacht' – the Irish speaking areas have been under a lot of pressure in the twenty first century, as old people die and younger people emigrated or moved to bigger cities, where employment prospects were more plentiful. Many others will say they hated the way Irish was taught in the schools, although that seems to have improved considerably. Nowadays parents, not Irish speakers themselves are opting to raise their children through Irish. Many more are going to evening Irish classes and there is a massive demand for Gael scoileanna (Irish-medium public schools) all over the country. Irish speakers and Gaeltacht locations are now cool and sexy. TG4 (Irish Language TV) delivers news, current affairs, weather, documentaries and all types of sports coverage in Irish from GAA and Rugby to the Tour de France. Parents from all across the country send their children to the Gaeltacht for the summer months to Irish summer colleges to improve their Irish Language skills and proficiency. Galway, Kerry and Donegal are winning All Irelands with many Irish speakers from Gaeltacht areas on their teams. Others are making it on to big stages in music, art and literature.

Exam results in Gaeltacht secondary schools are among the best in the country. I have spent the last ten or more years living away from where I was born. I miss the ocean and the shoreline on the Connemara Coast where I often strolled along in the early morning mist listening to the cleansing sound of the sea hitting the rocks. The dynamic power of those waves on a stormy day and the absolute beauty of the sunrise on the horizon. The backdrop of the commanding mountains and the Twelve Bens. A thoroughly magical place constantly changing and offering up a new dilemma and a different experience every time. Therapeutic landscapes as it is referred to. I also miss the people, especially the older wiser generation with the welcome smile and a quick turn of phrase. I have moved on, planted new seeds and my life is very different now. I am older and wiser; I have learnt from my past and from my experiences. For a couple of years there were many painful memories for me when I headed west across the Corrib. Plenty of reminders of projects I completed, site-works and excavation contracts I was involved with. Many roads and foundations for one off-houses and building projects I planned and brought to fruition. I am immensely proud of where I was born and who I have become. I have grown to accept and appreciate my achievements, and I have gained an understanding of what went wrong and the mistakes I made along the way. When you lose a business (or two), your livelihood and your marriage, you're thrown into a fierce violent hurricane, a personal tornado. You feel like your whole identity has deserted you. You are unable to plant your feet on any solid ground. It's very much like being stuck in quicksand.

Living on the edge of Europe where the next bit of land is three thousand miles away in the USA can be the same. It's beautiful and unique and picturesque and full of colour and vibrancy and then it can become stormy and violent, dark and strange. Connemara at the extreme end of Europe where the sweet and the bitter are blended. The author and artist Tim Robinson spent a few years in the area saying Connemara "a landscape in which beauty and suffering wrap closely around one another, and in which geology and mythology fuse together as – systems of description of what

22

can be seen in terms of what lies too deep to be seen" – Tim Robinson. For me, no matter where I go or find myself, "the ocean thunders in my bones" - It is a big part of my identity.

Chapter 3

I ALWAYS STOOD OUT FROM THE CROWD

I was once referred to as an "Emotional Lightning Rod" who -'feels the world more intensely'. I now believe that this statement is indeed a true reflection of me. I have the natural ability to light up a room and also to be intensely aware of what is going on for others in any given situation. This can be a blessing and a curse until you develop a mechanism to handle it. If you are a lightning rod you attract stuff to yourself in a particular order to shield others attention, criticism, controversy etc. Being an emotional lightning rod, you attract and absorb powerful and especially negative or hostile opinions etc, sometimes diverting such feelings from other targets. With experience I have developed a way of not taking stuff on board in a personal manner especially when it relates to others.

Success and achievements started to come my way early in life. I was making a mark. With the passing of my dad at such a young age it was inevitable that I would come under someone's influence other than my mother's. She had her hands full raising five children, running a shop and B&B. That came to pass when a local man who had returned from the UK (Huddersfield) to settle in his hometown of Carraroe came into my life. He built a supermarket and a café right beside the national school. Pádraic Kelly had a telling influence on my life as a young lad and well into my twenties. He had a great career as a player at home and in Huddersfield. Shortly after settling in the local community, he became involved in the local GAA club and became a central part of its progression. I hugely respected him, and I always felt he believed in me one hundred percent. His care and attention mattered a great deal in those years, and I always wanted to do and be my best for him in return. He had a commanding presence and a reputation as someone not to be messed with but could also be very jovial and full of life. He put in a word for me to get summer work on building sites with Údarás na Gaeltachta (the Gaeltacht development authority) and I know he did the same for other young men who were playing with the club at that time. He loved Don Williams and Merle Haggard among other country greats. When I chill out with a few whiskies I always listen to Don and Merle and fondly remember Pádraic. I will never forget his influence and the time he took to help me in those early years. He was a huge part of my life and I suppose a role model when I needed one. I firmly believe he was a guiding hand and a positive influence on me at a time when I was a vulnerable young man. Having had this experience, myself where someone took a big interest in me as a young lad and into my teens, guiding me and pushing me, encouraging and correcting me when I needed it, I will strongly encourage others to do the same if they have the pedigree and the character to do so. Unfortunately, what we get nowadays is the over-the-top pushy parent, father, or mother. I experienced plenty of this type of individual when managing teams at underage level and even worse still as a referee for youth matches.

Parenting has changed so much, especially in the last twenty years or so. Parents have become hugely involved in their children's lives, in many cases putting a lot of pressure on their kids to attain the best results and attend the best schools and colleges. The same applies to a child's participation in sports or other pass times. Playing a sport can help improve a child's self-esteem. Because it takes physical, mental and emotional endurance to compete, children learn motivation, determination and the long-term benefits of training and working towards a goal. The feeling of accomplishment as they work to build and develop their athletic skills improves self-esteem, a hugely important trait to face other challenges in life. Parents and coaches have a huge part to play in a child's development at this crucial early time in their lives. The emphasis and expectations need to be balanced. Learning and enjoyment must be to the forefront as children participate and learn leadership abilities and resilience. Parents need to find the middle ground between a permissive style and being overly protective. Coaches must be aware of the influence they will have on a young person's life and help them navigate through the process of learning, training and competing. Parents and coaches should be role models, therefore their attitude towards officials, the opposition and teammates should always be of the highest order and exhibit positive sportsmanship. Excessive pressure to perform and excel in sport especially can cause children to respond with anxiety and fears of inadequacy. If a child becomes overly dependent on the advice and guidance of parents, he/she may develop issues with self-confidence and feeling capable for success. The young person may protect themselves from a fear of failure by not taking chances or trying new things. Overprotective parents can protect a child to the point where he/she never learns how to persevere and keep trying when obstacles and challenges occur.

In my own experience my involvement in sport from a very early age curtailed my aggression and rebellion. It helped me with my self-esteem and self-confidence. It also taught me self-discipline and responsibility. Learning and developing these skills at an early age provides a great foundation for the future. Parents want to provide their kids with a rich, full childhood, and to have what they may not have had in some cases. Some try to relive their own childhood through their children. Some are competitive and want to keep up or undo relatives, neighbours, or friends. You surely know one of these people or you may be one yourself? Are you bringing your princess to ballet or music lessons because she wants to go or to keep up with other Mums? Do you want your son or daughter to go to a particular college so you can boast about it to your friends? Consider your own motives. Not every child is meant to be an athlete. Their talents may be in art, music or other areas. Allow your child to have fun and try different activities and discover his/her likes and dislikes. The individual talents will surface in due course. When parents assume the responsibility for controlling a child's behaviour and actions, the child misses the opportunity to develop these internal skills of self-discipline that help in various situations. They also miss the experience of self-motivation, decision making and responsibility. I love the way Pat Shortt the comedian brings this issue to light in his skit about a young student in the school – "Tommy is talking about going off to America and he can't even find his way home from the school gate". Can your child make their own way to or from the school gate or to anywhere else? Or is this simple task totally reliant on you as a parent to bring your child here there and everywhere? Are you contributing to molding your young child into a self-sufficient competent person able to make plans and decisions and take responsibility for themselves?

I had a conversation about this with my mother recently. At eighty-five years of age, she has experienced and seen many changes in our culture and society. As a wife on two occasions, a mum of seven, a grandmother and great grandmother, I respect and value her thoughts and comments, especially on worldly matters. It can be difficult to get her views as she is inclined to keep them to herself and just get on with life. "Children and teenagers are suffering the effects of over parenting" she strongly maintains.

We continue the chat, and she gets slightly animated after I delve a bit more. What do you mean? I asked. "Kids are not given the room or space to develop their natural ability to cope, to figure things out and deal with problems on their own. Decisions and solutions are constantly being made for them. They are not getting the opportunity to process loss or failure and come up with coping mechanisms. They are being ferried to and from school and every other event. At the mere sight of a problem or issue a parent is summoned into action". Helicopter parents!

As I grew up my mother was definitely not too involved in my life. I was encouraged to manage myself and my decisions, my triumphs and adversities and I strongly believe I was the better for it. This gave me a great foundation in my early years. I learned that I had to behave and perform and learn skills to better myself. I dealt with disappointments and learned from bad decisions. I appreciated earning a wage and I welcomed and accepted training and advice. I learned to respect others, I also learned from those I looked up to and valued their contributions to my life. Through my participation in sport, I saw the importance of preparation and practice and being a team member. I learned to cope with defeat and success in equal measure. I never felt under pressure, I enjoyed whatever I decided to do. I took responsibility for myself at an early age. Nothing was a problem, and I always achieved the goals I set for myself. I remained humble and respectful yet driven and determined. Laziness did not feature on my horizon there was no space for it! I looked it up in the Oxford dictionary - 'unwilling to work or be active, doing as little as possible'- that definitely will not make its way onto my gravestone!

I read a report recently that new research has found that parents are now scared that today's teens lack basic skills and can't cope with stress, budgeting or even a broken heart. In a survey conducted by the National Citizen Service – twenty thousand mums and dads said they feared their teens lacked essential skills on both a practical and emotional level. The following is a short list of the life skills their teens are lacking: 1) How to deal with stress. 2) How to budget. 3) How to deal with a broken heart. 4) How to save money. 5) How to pay bills. 6) How to drive. 7) How to look after yourself on a night out. 8) How to be independent. 9) How to build self-esteem. 10) How to clean a toilet. 11) Resilience. 12) How to eat a balanced diet. 13) How to fold clothes/sheets properly. 14) How to be polite. 15) How to make the bed properly! The list goes on - I decided not to show my mother, she'd have a conniption!!

Padraic Kelly thought me the importance of showing up before time, to make my own way when possible (usually on a bicycle) to work hard on my skills and fitness. To push myself to improve and work on my weaknesses. He also inspired me to be ruthless in competition, magnanimous in victory and gracious in defeat. Outside the sporting arena this man instilled in me an ethos of good character, with traits of honesty, humility, responsibility and selflessness. Learning these skills at a young age is a brilliant bedrock for life itself and have stood to me ever since. I worked in An Chistín Bar and Óstán An Cheathrú Rua for a couple of summers and during Easter and other holidays. Both establishments were owned by my Uncle Peter O Shea. He operated these two businesses' and was ably assisted for many years by his Manager Bartley Reaney. I really enjoyed the buzz of working in these environments. An Chistín was a live music pub with a brilliant atmosphere especially during the summer months with live bands seven nights a week for tourists and locals. The hotel hosted many weddings for the surrounding areas as well as christenings, birthday celebrations and funerals. For many years it was frequented by tourists holidaying in the Connemara region. I loved the variety of working in both places at the same time. I learned loads from Bartley Reaney about tidiness, cleanliness, serving customers, punctuality, teamwork, attention to detail and good personal grooming. From this culture and also being brought up in my home where we ran a shop and a B and B, I appreciated the ethos and the ethics involved in serving the public and working in the hospitality industry.

I spent a few summers working in the Galway Metal Company as I got a bit older. This was totally different to what I had been doing and learning up until now. It was my first introduction to the world of trucks and heavy machinery. An area where I later went on to become very successful and make a lot of money. My uncles, Colm and Bill worked there and decided to bring me in for a bit of experience. Officially my job was to paint up the machinery and anything else that needed painting around the depots. I loved it. Before long I was loading and unloading the trucks, segregating various types of material and feeding scrap into the baling machines and the car crushers. Some days I went out in the trucks collecting loads of scrap with the drivers, calling to private individuals, garages and commercial premises to remove their unwanted or discarded scrap materials. Travelling to Galway Metal with the men was a great experience for me at the time. They drove beautiful cars were always slagging one another and playing tricks. Paddy Walsh owned Galway Metal that time with two depots in

Prospect Hill in the City and Oranmore on the outskirts of Galway. Paddy had known and lived through very hard times before becoming very wealthy. He employed a large contingent from the Carraroe area. He treated me very well, paid me well as a young teen and gave me the scope to try out different things. Every Friday evening Paddy paid all his employees at his office. He drove top of the range BMW's and was always impeccably dressed in white shirts, ties and top-quality suits. With a glint in his eye, he would ask me every single time "did you get much painting done this week Máirtín?" He knew very well I was doing very little painting and much more machine driving. He slowly counted out my wages with crispy notes and there always seemed to be plenty of them. As a young teenager I loved the whole ritual and the importance he put upon paying me and thanking me for my great work. Most weeks he would add in a bonus. I was on top of the world, Paddy respected me and I always did my best for him. Years later I always treated my own employees in the same way. In hindsight now, I most definitely agree that the lessons I learned in those early years of my life molded me into the person I became. The respect, determination and mindset to push myself, I learned from Pádraic Kelly. The time keeping, the importance of cleanliness/tidiness and responsibility and treating customers with respect from my uncle Peter and his manager, Bartley Reaney. The respect, organisational skills and the will to just get on with things regardless of circumstances I learned from Tess – my Mother. You can come through very difficult times and personal circumstances and be successful, and treat your employees with respect and dignity – I picked up that lesson from Paddy Walsh

You pick this up because it's instilled in you by the good people you meet and their influence on you as you travel along your journey. Life Lesson: If you can have a positive, constructive, informative, influence on young people of any age, always do so. What I learned from these influential people at an early stage in my life has stood to me much more than anything I ever learned at school. I was always amazed at those who were self-taught with little or in some case's hardly any education. These people were gifted individuals who all played some part in my life, and it was such a privilege to spend time in their company. Each and every one of them enriched my life in many ways.

My schooling finished at secondary level after the Leaving Certificate. I was bright and intelligent but not academic. One of my English teachers in secondary school was consistently on my case. She loved my imagination

29

and the way I wrote essays but informed me regularly that I was wasting my talents with other interests outside the school. I was spending a lot of time with sporting activities-Gaelic football in particular. My mother had remarried at this stage and my stepfather Michael was running a truck and machinery business. I got stuck into this at every opportunity, helping him out and driving the trucks at a very young age. My intention was to join the Garda Síochána after leaving school. I did the entrance exam in 1979, got the call afterwards but decided to stay at the trucks and machinery. Had I become a Garda at that time I would be retired now with a nice pension. But of course, I would not have had the same life experiences that has provided me with the content for this book. Sport has played a big part in my life from my early childhood. I captained the national school Gaelic football team, and we won a Connemara schools competition on two occasions. I also captained the local club team at many levels during my career going on to train and manage at Underage, Junior, Intermediate and Senior Level. I was comfortable being a leader and always lead by example. I joined the local Boxing Club for the winter months to keep in shape in the off season. It helped my confidence and taught me how to handle pain. It made me more disciplined and more patient. My co-ordination and endurance improved as did my core and overall fitness levels. When facing an opponent in the ring you learn how to control fear and you become humbler. I won some fights and lost some as-well. There's nothing like a black eye, bloody nose and sore ribs to build humility. The toughness needed to fight also exposes you to the fragility of human life. You learn how easy it is to damage a human being. You develop respect and empathy for people's pain. You appreciate the body's ability to persist against difficulty and the mental fortitude required to continue in the face of pain. When you fight a person who is trained to hurt you, the rest of your fears seem small in comparison. As in boxing, learning to persevere through your fears and staying committed to your goals can completely change your life, as I have found out on many occasions in my business and also in my sporting challenges. I took up athletics for a few years in secondary school. Middle distance running the 800 and 1,500 metres were my best events. Father Tommy Mannion trained us in the school and encouraged us to enter schools' competitions at local and regional events. I became a Connacht Champion at the Long Jump which became my main focus at the time. I loved the variety and testing myself at different disciplines. In the summer months Carraroe was always busy with students based in Colaiste Columba for four-week courses to improve their Irish.

The Colaiste (Irish speaking college) was actually set up by my mother and a group of local ladies who joined forces and set up a co-op and got the very successful college up and running. Students came from all over the country and based themselves with local families in their respective homes and attended the college for the duration of their stay. It was a very lucrative business for the local community and the Bean an Tí (meaning woman of the house or landlady who takes in students to her home). While the students are in the house learning Irish this lady was really the star of the show. Feeding and looking after the students and acting as mother, guardian and disciplinarian and everything in between. The students attended classes in the morning, going back to their lodgings for lunch and the afternoon was normally spent at the local beaches or playing sport at the Colaiste. Dinner was served between five and six o clock and back to the local 'halla' for the ceilí. I got to know Bernie O Connell one of the regular teachers whose brief also included running sporting activities for the students during their stay. We came up with an idea that it would be super cool for a team made up of local lads to take on the best players from each course over the three months. We decided on four sports. Gaelic football – soccer – volleyball – basketball. The rivalry was fierce. The college students were roared on by enthusiastic supporters, all fellow students of course. The atmosphere was always electric with hundreds attending all the events. We usually played warm up matches for the first few weeks of each course, heading to a crescendo and a big weekend of events before the students went away. This 'big weekend' finished with a celebratory ceilí for all. Many 'first kisses' were initiated at these nights and some crushes were acted upon. Being a player for the local lads put us in the limelight and being a handy dancer added to my own credentials. I truly loved those summers and the fun and excitement we had. Apologies to those on the receiving end of some sloppy kissing! Walking the girl's home was really tricky because the Bean an Tí was always watching out for her students and especially getting them home indoors on time for supper before curfew. My bicycle was a valued companion for bringing a cailín (young lady) to the house she was staying in. If you got her on the cross bar, you were elected, and it was easier to deviate to a local beach or a quiet spot for a proper snog and a chat! All this was done to teach the girls a bit more Irish to improve their command of the language of course. We were never really heart broken when the buses collected all the students and brought them away to Galway to catch trains and expressway coaches as they headed home to their various destinations at the end of their stay in the Gaeltacht, because usually the same day or following day a new bunch arrived in town for the next course. It was great to get the chance to play different sports during the summer months and experience the thrill of competing against students from all over the country while being watched by hundreds of screaming fans. The only game I regret not having played is hurling. It was not played in our area at the time. Ironically, I now live in Kinvara where hurling is very strong and most conversations centre around the small ball, known as the sliotar. I spent the first forty or so years of my life heavily involved in the GAA and especially my own club in Carraroe. While I enjoyed playing up until I sustained a career ending injury, I got huge satisfaction out of coaching and managing club teams.

At adult level I was a man manager and always worked closely with the individuals. Often helping players with any personal matters that might affect their commitment or performance when required to do so. Anything from cutting out bad habits or improving time keeping and addressing work related constraints. It improved their performance and overall quality of life. I also worked with youngsters at underage level. I enjoyed helping them develop and always instilled a learning manner with fun and respect and good sportsmanship at its core. I am now fully qualified as a Life Coach more than twenty years later to professionally do what I was actually doing back in those days. Sports people and athletes work extremely hard to reach their potential within their chosen sport, to be able to perform at their best. Life coaching, I believe, can assist them with their self-management, goal setting, limiting beliefs, untangling fears, identifying obstacles and other draining habits. As a Life Coach I help give a person the confidence to believe in themselves and their skills so that they can achieve whatever it is they set their minds to. As a sportsman, mountaineer and endurance athlete I have attained many goals and completed many challenges to date. However, I have suffered with confidence issues myself in my own challenges, whether in business or sport. In many ways sport and life are very similar. You learn to be a leader or a follower. You learn that mistakes happen and how to overcome them. You learn how to deal with obstacles and overcome them. You have to know how to formulate and execute a game plan. You learn how to lose and that things don't always go to plan. You accept that you have to plan and prepare, set and achieve your goals. Winning and success are not a given. It takes constant hard work and dedication.

I Always Stood Out from the Crowd

We now live in a world where efficiency and top-class performance is demanded as much as it is expected more than ever. Companies are trying to manage talent effectively to achieve organisational business objectives, regardless of industry, staff size or location. The emphasis is on how to improve employee performance, based on steps to take and rules to follow. I think this approach is bonkers and giving the wrong message entirely. Social media platforms are chock a block with information and strategies for leaders and companies to get the best structures in place to get staff to the new level now required when coming back to work. What a load of bollocks. It's the same as getting the team into the dressing room in Croke Park for the All Ireland Final and expecting them to perform at their best because that's what is required and expected. Or bringing a team to the Olympics and expecting gold medal performances with new rules and regulations and targets. Huge portions of society are struggling to some degree. I see it every week in my coaching practice. People are carrying mental and emotional injuries. They need and want to be heard. They are not fit to go back doing the same thing they did before Covid and all that has happened. Employees are exiting a very turbulent time in their lives for most, after the last eighteen months. They want to see changes in how they are being dealt with. Many are instigating changes in their own personal lives, more are changing careers and deciding to 'live a better life' to attain a better balance.

"Yesterday I was clever, so I wanted to change the world.
Today I am wise, so I am changing myself" - Rumi, Persian poet.

Every single person at all levels is dealing with change to some degree or other. Some have felt the experience in a traumatic way, anxiety, stress and depression levels have increased and things remain uncertain. The fear of becoming infected and the lockdown measures drastically changed people's daily routines. From my own experience of uncertainty and upheaval and life being turned on its head, I know the importance of mental and physical wellbeing. Mindset clearly comes into play. Panic behaviour or hysteria and feelings of hopelessness and desperation must be controlled. Adjusting to a global or personal crisis or a bit of both by building resilience can help you cope with the stress. Living through tough times can take a heavy toll on your mood, health and outlook. You may be grieving all that you've lost, flooded by difficult conflicting emotions or uncertain how to move on with your life. Like me you may feel your life is totally out of control and you feel powerless and unable to affect whatever happens next. Sometimes there is no way to avoid the sorrow, adversity and distress of life. Resilience does help you cope with these troubling times and helps you bounce back from hardship, loss and tragedy. It takes time to build however as I will mention in depth in Chapter 6. Unless you've faced adversity in your life before, it's unlikely you've had the need or opportunity to develop resilience. Accepting the situation is where you start, denial is not the answer. Focus next on what you can control, take strength from difficult things you have coped with in the past, accept your feelings and process them, allow yourself to grieve. Reach out to others or a professional person. Stay away from negative people and invest in self-care (very important). Exercise and pursue some hobbies. Practice relaxation and aim to improve your sleep.

Stay motivated, eat well and celebrate small wins. Deal with your issues one small step at a time. Express gratitude for positive things and people in your life, maintain a hopeful outlook and last but not least be kind to yourself. Business leaders and company owners must get to know their people, their team members. Meet them where they are at in their own personal lives, not in the dressing room. Helping people at a personal level to handle their own problems is my goal. Only by doing this can we improve their performance, their quality of life, their physical and mental health and by extension their work, career and sporting endeavours. People are reaching out and reevaluating their lives and setting new goals. If you are one of these people you have the chance to abandon old habits and behaviours and take up new ones. Have a look through your rucksack and discard what is no longer relevant. Get out of the autopilot manner in which you were operating in the past. Take the wheel of your own life, 'it's your story'- reconsider your priorities and enjoy your liberation.

"The difference between stumbling blocks and steppingstones is how you use them."

Chapter 4

WITH FIRE & PASSION I TOOK THE CHALLENGE

Thursday October 5th2000. – Location San Diego, California,USA.

Time 4.30am and still dark outside. It is 12.30pm at home, we are eight hours behind Ireland. I had not slept well. A mix of nervous excitement and apprehension. Our room was hot and stuffy. My mind was racing all night, had I prepared well enough? Had I enough miles in my legs? Had I trained properly? Did I make the correct equipment choices?

What equipment? My bike frame/wheels/tyres/tubes/saddle/seat post/handlebars/pedals/cleats/chain rings/gear ratios/ What about my clothing? The most important decision of all perhaps, my cycling shorts. Did I choose the best brand and quality and the most appropriate for me to avoid potential saddle sores? Would my choice of rain gear protect me enough in bad weather? 'Relax man or you'll give yourself a seizure. You have prepared well and you are in super shape to take on this event and you have researched and tested and very carefully selected every single piece of equipment and clothing. "You'll be grand, just chill the feck out", I said to myself.

My breathing slowed, I began to relax again and appreciate the magic of just stretching out on a comfortable bed and imagining this wonderful adventure that lay ahead for us. 32 cyclists and 15 support crew from all over the island of Ireland who had signed up for this "Ultimate Challenge"- USA 3,000 miles Coast to Coast Cycle Challenge. My thoughts began to wander. Our journey was to bring us across ten states. From the Pacific Coast all the way to the Atlantic Ocean. A chance in a lifetime to experience the awesome vastness of America. Our route is recognised as the Southern Transcontinental. We begin our tour by crossing the mountains and deserts of South California into Arizona and New Mexico, over the Rocky Mountains across Texas with all its oil fields, Arkansas, Mississippi with the largest river in the US, Alabama, Tennessee (the birthplace of country music) over the

Appalachian Mountains across Georgia and on to the finish line in South Carolina. WOW, what an incredible experience this will be.

I am chuffed to have, at least, made it to the start line in San Diego. To have secured sponsorship and exceeded the fundraising target of ten thousand pounds. To have completed the gruelling training programme and preparation that was required for this "Ultimate Challenge". This reminds me one of my main sponsors are RTE Radio na Gaeltachta. (Irish Language radio station). A condition of this support is that I must do regular live interviews for the station and its many listeners. The first interview is today, this morning! One of my early teachers in primary school said it was good to "dream big".

"All our dreams can come true, if we have the courage to pursue them". - Walt Disney.

You set a goal and with that you explore your abilities to accomplish your goal successfully. Your abilities enable you to handle many challenges in your life. I had set and accomplished many goals in my life. This was a massive endurance event. Billed as "The Ultimate Challenge".

A fundraiser for the National Council for the Blind of Ireland (NCBI), under the NCBI umbrella, the "Blazing Saddles" were formed to raise funds through cycling challenges and sponsorship. I heard about the event towards the latter end of 1999, I was completing many different charity cycles around the country at this stage but nothing on the scale or magnitude of the USA challenge. What I was doing for a few years was considered 'leisure cycling', but this challenge would require a big step up to elite level. In January 2000, I attended the official launch of the event by Mike Sullivan, the American Ambassador to Ireland, at his residence in the Phoenix Park and signed the contract. I was now fully committed and motivated.

I began to up my training and increased the time I was spending on my bike. Included in the detailed contract documents we all signed was a rule that we all must participate in a full training programme assessment and medical testing on two occasions. Early in our preparations and again about four to six weeks before we were due to head away. This was critical. Firstly, it was immediately evident what our fitness levels were and if we had any underlying yet unknown medical conditions. Having completed these tests, a training programme was individually designed for every member of the Blazing Saddles USA Coast to Coast team, including how to use and train with a heart rate monitor. The tests were carried out at the Institute for Sport and Human Performance at Trinity College in Dublin city. The Director of the Human Performance Lab was Bernard Donne a man of few words but with the ability to 'cut through the shit' and call a spade exactly what it is. They usually dealt with elite athletes. The test is a grilling really, where you are pushed to your actual limits and your data is assessed. After all the preliminary medical checks are completed and you fill out a very detailed questionnaire you position yourself on a bike. You are then wired up like something resembling spaghetti junction, a mask is tightly fitted to your face and you start to pedal keeping the pedal stroke at a specific cadence as pressure is increased. Bernard then lances the tip of your finger with a blade before the start of the test. The purpose of all of this is to determine your VO2 max and your threshold levels. The mask measures metabolic data, including oxygen consumption and respiratory exchange rates. A small sample of blood is taken from your fingertip every two minutes approximately to measure lactate levels. The increase of lactate levels in the blood are an indicator of fatigue. Your threshold is established where the body switches from working aerobically to anaerobically. Increasing your lactate tolerance plays a crucial role in improving your fitness levels. The VO2 max is the amount of oxygen consumed per kilo of body mass. I lasted 23 minutes before being told to pedal slowly and cool down for a few minutes and then have a shower as I was dripping in sweat from the effort. I was among the best performers from the team in this initial test. For many others the timing was less than 18 minutes. While my timing was good in comparison with most of the team, I was nowhere near where I needed to be for such a gruelling endurance challenge.

Defining your Lactate Threshold (LT) and VO2 max numbers help you train more efficiently and improve your performance. During exercise, lactate naturally flows into your bloodstream as your body attempts to increase the breakdown of glucose for energy production. As intensity increases and energy demands can no longer be met entirely with aerobic energy systems, blood lactate begins to rise and prevent that intensity from being sustained for very long. If you train your body to better withstand more intense exercise, you'll be able to perform longer and harder. That is why Lactate Threshold is so important. VO2 max is defined by the maximum volume of oxygen per minute that an athlete can capture from the air, fix at pulmonary level, transport and utilize. This level can also be improved and developed with the correct training.

I felt fecked as I showered, but also excited to get my results from Bernard and a full report on how my body was performing. He greeted me with a straight face holding reams of paper and a pen. I sat down in front of him like a bold child in front of the headmaster. "What type of training are you doing?" he asked. I proceeded to give him a blow by blow account of the previous ten or so weeks since signing up for this challenge. "If you keep that up", he said "you will last about three days in America!! This is what you need to do and how you have to do it while using a heart rate monitor as much as possible". He spent the next thirty minutes going through charts and heart rate zones, training peaks, nutrition, hydration and so on with me.

I learned a very valuable lesson that day in Trinity. I had to train to a plan and watch the numbers along with my diet and hydration. It has stood to me for many challenges in the last twenty plus years. Another condition of the contract was that all training camps organised by the NCBI were compulsory. Every month over the next ten months we all gathered together in some part of Ireland for two or three training days at a time. This was invaluable as we got to know each other, trained and socialised together and got used to cycling together. Initially 34 cyclists were signed up and training for the USA Coast to Coast.

After each camp you got a very in-depth indication as to where your own fitness levels were compared to others in the group and this often resulted in people increasing their own work rates and trying to keep in step with everyone else. As we had five cyclists from Galway involved, we began to train together, doing 150/200 mile spins at weekends and mid-week, steadily building up the training miles while doing so at a high level of intensity.

Seán Kelly had retired from the professional peloton in 1994. He was and still is to this day one of the most successful road cyclists of all time. Seán became a Team Leader and Technical Director with the "Blazing Saddles" for the NCBI after retiring. He worked with the organisation for this tour, designing the training camps and the actual stages in America. He gave insightful information to us and motivational talks and his presence was a huge boost to all of us. To have someone of his calibre, pedigree and success as a team leader was very inspirational. The ex GAA county footballer with the dodgy knee was in the middle of all of this! I was learning loads about the body, the mindset, strengths and weaknesses. I was averaging 200/500 miles a week and spending hours upon hours in the saddle. I lost a power of weight. My bodyweight had dropped by more than a stone and a half

(10kgs). My percentage of body fat had also come down from a chubby 21% to just under 10%, my cadence and power output improved immeasurably, as did my bike handling skills. Seán Kelly tells a story of our first meeting at one of the early training camps in Carrick On Suir. I took a banana out of my pocket and tried to peel it back to consume it while on the move and ended up in a heap in the middle of the road! He does maintain that I became one of his better pupils. I became adept at cycling stuff. Bike handling, cadence and power output, drafting in a group, measuring my effort on big climbs, conserving my energy and controlling my effort on long stages, holding the wheel in front, getting out of the saddle while keeping the bike in forward momentum, riding at paceline, descending (fast), cornering and awareness of the appropriate pedal position, bumping (shoulders/elbows), looking behind, eating/drinking, riding comfortably with no hands (while taking off/putting on a rain cape/gillet) and the one I am most proud of – I learned to pee off the bike while in motion (most cyclists never master that)!!The whole team headed back to Trinity for final testing in late August and early September 2000. It was discovered that two of the group had developed underlying conditions and would therefore not be travelling. They were devastated having put in a big effort with their health status only coming to light for them at this late stage in the training regime. That meant we now had thirty two cyclists for the challenge.

I rocked up for my tests in September and I knew what to expect this time. I lasted only twenty-nine minutes on the bike – six minutes more than the last time in February! I showered and sat down again in front of Mr. Donne. "How do you feel?" he said. "To be honest I am devastated, I responded – almost a year of hard training and I only lasted an extra six minutes?" He smiled and laughed and held up the paperwork in his right hand and dropped it to the desk. "textbook results" he exclaimed. "You obviously trained as per your programme and followed the plan. We put your body under intense pressure this time and it responded very well to the demands. All your scores have improved immensely. Barring accident or illness you will have no bother cycling across America. "I sat back in the chair and was overcome with a feeling of elation and satisfaction. Like what you get when you're rewarded for putting in a great effort. Now ALL I had to do was go and actually cycle the three thousand miles in twenty-five days and not get sick or have an accident, which was completely another story.

Apologies for the next paragraph if you are not a 'cycling head'. But some will have a keen interest in my choices.

I had just upgraded my bike so I would get used to it for a couple of weeks before our trip. I purchased a TREK carbon fibre frame with Rolf Vector wheels and dura ace groupset. A Selle Royal saddle. I opted for Continental Gator Skin 25mm tyres and tubes. They are bullet proof for mileage and no punctures. I was using AESOS Bib Shorts and found them brilliant for long hours in the saddle. I had tried and tested all gear and equipment and I had changed and found what I liked and what I found most beneficial and comfortable. This was not a Sunday spin we were going for after all. My total training mileage for this challenge was in excess of six thousand miles. Many of those long arduous miles I completed on my own. My training arena was Connemara. Many of the long routes I completed were in excess of two hundred miles, taking in picturesque, breathtaking mountain scenery and beautiful rugged coastline. While the training environment was indeed beautiful and stunning it was also equally the hardest and harshest you could imagine. I did not have to deal with traffic, or traffic lights, or big towns and cities, bus lanes or angry or stressed-out drivers. Connemara gets more than a fair share of strong winds and rain, extreme weather if you like. Living in this part of Ireland on the west coast you build up a form of acceptance and tolerance of these conditions. Training and riding a bicycle in them bring plenty of challenges. Being situated on the extreme west coastline narrows your route options to begin with, you can go South, East, or North but not West. The golden rule of a cycling spin is to head out against the wind and home with the wind to your back if possible. As you are getting tired on your return you have the benefit of the wind to your backside. Not always easy to manage this based in Connemara. The landscape is barren, there are no trees or hedges along the roadways for protection and shelter. The road surfaces are heavy and un-relenting with no roll off them for your wheels. This is 'hard territory' to train in. The Atlantic Ocean has many moods, the most familiar being a punishing sadistic one. Storms batter the west coast from autumn to spring and the wind never drops below a strong breeze. Hard man territory but the best training conditions for any endurance event. Character Building without a shadow of a doubt. Every time I went out, I was testing myself and pushing myself against the elements and surroundings. My tolerance levels were improving. I was spending many hours on my own battling wind and rain, building my resilience and fitness and most importantly my mental strength. There was no place to hide. Bike handling in the wind and rain also improved.

When the Galway contingent of the USA Coast to Coast team trained together it was mostly in Connemara for the same reasons.

Monday October 2nd, 2000.

Our flight with Continental Airlines departed Dublin for Los Angeles and a connecting flight to San Diego. We landed at 7.30pm local time (8hrs behind Ireland) with a 20-minute transfer to our hotel – the Best Western on Circle Drive. This was our base to rest, relax and prepare for the next 2 days. After putting our bikes together, the next day Wednesday October 3rd, a few of us went for a short spin to make sure the bike saddle height, handlebar position, gear changing, and tyre pressures were all in order. We enjoyed a relaxing lunch on the coast and wondered with excitement what lay ahead. I don't know what a well-trained and prepared racehorse feels like before an event, but I felt like I was in the shape of my life for the hardest challenge imaginable. San Diego is a large city on the Pacific Ocean in the state of California and adjacent to the Mexican border. Known for its beaches, parks and warm climate. A deep harbour is home to a large active naval fleet, with the USS Midway an aircraft – carrier – turned museum open to the public. Some other team members arranged to take a bus to the Mexican Border. We had some media work to get through, team photo shoots interviews and so on. I also had my own media work with my main sponsors RTE Radio na Gaeltachta. My other main sponsor was Curleys Quality Foods, Castlegar, Galway.

John Curley, the owner was so impressed with the idea of cycling a bike across America he immediately volunteered to become a main sponsor. On Wednesday evening October 4th we had a ceremonial dipping of the wheels in the Pacific Ocean with the thought that the next dip of the wheels would be in the Atlantic three thousand miles later. No pressure!!

I was sharing a room with John Mannion for the duration of our tour. We had shared a room for all the preparation and training during the year. John, a very prominent publican in Galway City had broken his collarbone in a cycling crash only seven weeks before we headed for the USA. We were training in a group and he touched a wheel in front of him and came down hard on the road. Being so close to such a gruelling event we all thought that was the end of the dream for him. Not John. He had an operation on his fractured clavicle which involved an open incision to move bone fragments into proper position and then secure them in place by attaching a plate with screws to the outside bone. Normal recovery time is twelve weeks. John had the procedure two weeks before the start of the event. After the fall the advice was to wait and let the swelling go down and then assess it. He was advised to wait a bit longer to see if it would start to knit back together. Time was running out and he was missing valuable training and preparation. He contacted Seán Kelly, who broke his collarbone on three occasions during his professional cycling career. They had a discussion and John decided to get a plate put in to have any chance of taking part in the challenge of cycling across America. It was a sign of his determination and willpower that he was at the start line in October 2000 having missed some valuable build up time. We got on very well which is extremely important when tackling such an endurance event. We are both organised and neat, good timekeepers and respectful of each other's space. For me John was a dream roommate. We became very close friends during those times and especially so during the event.

NOTE: *References - distance will be in miles and speed will be miles per hour and climbing will be in feet. Liquid consumption in gallons.*

STAGE 1 = SAN DIEGO – EL CENTRO CA   130 miles

After I finished my media interview with RTE Radio na Gaeltachta at 5am San Diego time (1pm in Ireland) I went for breakfast and then wished group 1 the best of luck as they headed away in darkness shortly after 6am. As a result of our training camps during the year and all the rider profiles and stats that had been gathered by the team management and Seán Kelly, it was decided to break up the thirty two cyclists into two groups. Group 1 now departing the Best Western Hotel was made up of the nucleus of the team and would depart about one hour each day for every stage before group 2. The strategy behind this was twofold. The riders in group 2 were able to consistently ride at a higher average speed and by sending group 1 away first every morning with group 2 steadily catching up after a few hours. It meant from a logistics and support point of view the teams were actually gradually coming together out on the road. It was thought it would also be good for morale. Cyclists had the option of moving from group to group depending on how you were feeling –strong –tired-injured-not recovering well - pissed off – depressed. Others would decide which group to cycle with based on the terrain – hilly –flat – undulating or the weather conditions – side winds – head winds – heavy rain – heat (high temps also brought problems). The groups had team leaders, Seán Kelly and Paul Butler a very experienced cyclist who represented Ireland at many international events. The lads would alternate between the groups as they saw fit.

At 7.15am on a chilly morning outside the Best Western on Hotel Circle Drive – I had a moment of contemplation. I blessed myself and said a wee prayer, to be safe and stay healthy and upright and enjoy this epic once in a lifetime journey. I clipped in to my pedals took a very deep breath and joined Group 2 consisting of twelve team members today, as we headed off on the 130 miles that lay ahead on the first stage of twenty five stages . We had light rain for 15 miles. The first section of the route today was undulating with a lot of drags and climbs. Stage 1 is rated as index 1 and one of the tougher stages, interstate highways with difficult entry and exit ramps, with a hard shoulder for most of the stage. We hit tough rolling hills at 25 miles accompanied by strong crosswinds. From 50 miles the terrain was mountainous and arid dessert and very hot! After the second food stop with just over 40 miles to go, the route took us up steep mountains with very fast descents and across the Yuhu Desert where the temperatures soared to 110degrees Fahrenheit (43degrees Celsius). I really struggled to finish the last 15 miles. I was cramping badly in both legs. I was not alone, many more suffered the same thing. Dehydration took a toll on many of us. Glad to get to our hotel for the night – The Ramada Inn El Centro CA. First bite taken out of the elephant!

I was still cramping up while getting a massage, I was badly dehydrated, I rested in the room for a few hours before dinner and drank gallons of water, loaded up on electrolytes and anti-cramp tablets, dioralyte and anything else I could find.

Cycling time – 7hrs 12 mins

Average 16.9 mph

STAGE 2 = El Centro CA – Yuma AZ   70 miles

One of the shortest stages of the challenge. It was planned that we would need a shorter stage after the difficult first stage to help us acclimatise and get our bodies accustomed to the demands of multi day stages in a different time zone with all kinds of weather and temperatures. Group 1 departed at 9.00am we headed off at 10.00.

Today we had one food stop. The catering team of Mick and Margaret Cowell travelled in an RV which was used every day as the main feeding station. Mick and Margaret prepared food for us on the stages. If the stage was less than 100 miles we had one food stop, if it was more than 100 miles we had two. The food stop RV / Mick and Margaret were such a welcome sight every day. Today was a very flat stage, really long stretches of road that seemed to go on forever, blistering heat in excess of 100degrees Fahrenheit and sand all around us as we made our way through the desert of the Algodones Dunes in the south-eastern portion of California near the border with Arizona and the Mexican border. We went through the small town of Felicity, the official "Centre of the World". The mood in the peloton was good with little conversation as the pace was high. We left California behind and entered the state of Arizona.

Hotel – Radisson Suites – Yuma AZ

Cycling time 3hrs 45 mins

Average 20 mph

Got a nice massage and had a good chat with John Mannion in our room before dinner.

He was doing really well even though his shoulder was extremely painful on some of the rougher road surfaces.

STAGE 3 = Yuma AZ - Gila Bend AZ   118 miles
Saturday October 7th, 2000.

Group 1 started today's stage at 6.00am we rolled out at 7am. Two food stops planned for 45 miles and 85 miles. We set a fast pace today averaging 21 mph. After some early short sharp climbs, we spent long periods on the freeway with some long stretches through the desert. Temperature again up at 105degrees Fahrenheit. For much of the stage we cycled beside a railway line with massively long trains with over a hundred freight carriages. Counting the carriages as they passed us became the thing to do to break up the monotony of the stage. Some of the drivers honking the train horns at us brought a feeling of appreciation. The soles of my feet felt on fire today and my toes sore from a combination of the extreme heat and the vibration from the road. For long distance cycling I found it helpful to get my cycling shoes a size bigger to allow room for the feet to swell especially in extreme heat. You can counter that in the cold by wearing two pairs of socks if you need to. After just over six hours of cycling we reached our destination in Gila Bend AZ , the Space Age Lodge/ Best Western Hotel. The hotel with the unusual theme lives up to its name. In order of importance after a stage we had the following rituals which we carried out every evening no matter what.

As soon as you get off the bike – food and re-hydration (usually energy drinks/jam sandwiches) – look at the list and time slots for massage (who was your masseur or soigneur - French word for carer) find your luggage and bring it to your room – shower – wash your gear in the shower - rest for a while if you didn't have an early massage time slot – more hydration/electrolyte drinks – next up wash and inspect your bike (tyres in particular for cuts or bulges) – any other bike issues talk to the mechanics – put your bike away in the lock up area if such a place was provided – do the laundry when available (John and I took turns to do each other's laundry while the other could got some much needed rest) – eat dinner – relaxation – few beers to help us unwind and sleep. That was it after every stage, and these duties would have to be performed religiously.

STAGE 4 = Gila Bend AZ - Globe AZ   150 miles
Sunday October 8th, 2000.

Group 1 departs at 6am

Group 2 departs at 6.45am – reduced to ten riders today. Declan Sugrue and Sé Weston opted to join group 1. This is a beast of a stage at 150 miles not helped by starting straight into a headwind. Plenty of sand and debris coming at us compliments of the strong winds and the Arizona deserts. Welcome foodstop at 45 miles. We push on as the winds reach 40 mph speeds and we get two torrential showers of rain. Man, this shit is hard!! At 95 miles shortly after the second foodstop we climb up over the Gonzales Pass. A tough climb with spectacular scenery. The views don't get any better after this but the climbs get worse. We are starting to hit the Rocky Mountains.

Most of the remaining 50 miles is uphill over 3,100 ft, we have already spent over 5 hours in the saddle. Trying to ride at a steady pace to keep our reduced group together and still make progress without overextending ourselves for the many days ahead. We were a very tired bunch, but happy to pull into the Days Inn in Globe AZ at the end of today's gruelling stage.

10.5 hours on the bike

5,540 ft of climbing

3 gallons of water consumed

11,040 calories burned! I will not require a sleeping tablet after that effort today.

STAGE 5 = Globe AZ - Show Lo AZ   85.5 miles
Monday October 9th,2000.

A shortish tough, hard, gruelling day. After breakfast the teams depart at 7.45am and 8.30am.

Our group 2 is further reduced to nine riders this morning. As we settle into a nice pace early on, we pass the Arizona State Prison and we push on for Salt River Canyon, a welcome sight and the location of our only food stop at 39 miles. As we are in the Rockies, the climbs today are steep and the views are breathtaking. The road surfaces are pretty good with very fast descents at 55-65 mph. At the bottom of one of the descents we encountered a State Trooper going ballistic! He had a speed gun and had clocked four of us (myself included) coming down the mountain at speeds in excess of 60 mph. Speed Limit on the descent was 40 mph. He was not impressed and threatened to pull our road pass for the day. In some states road passes for the particular roads or highways we were on needed to be purchased. For the entire trip 346 passes had to be purchased. The state trooper had to be bribed with Baileys, Irish Mist and promises. After giving us a good tongue wagging he let us continue. We are in Indian Country now as we pass through towns with names like Cedar Creek, Fort Apache, Cibique and Cedar Canyon Bridge. For the last 15 miles today we cycle through a lovely forest area, Tonto National Park with a cooling breeze and nice rolling flat roads.

5.5 hrs cycling time

8,300 ft of climbing. Our hotel this evening – Days Inn - dinner and breakfast at JB's restaurant next door. Five stages now completed - ONLY 20 to go! Or 556 miles done and a little over 2,445 miles still to get through. The 25 stages are made up like this...

6 days/stages = 140-160miles

5 days/stages = 130-140miles

9 days/stages = 120-130miles

5 days/stages = 58-120miles

After 20% of the event I feel physically and mentally strong and in good form. John Mannion is also getting stronger every day and our conversations off the bike are positive and constructive. We have made a conscious decision not to discuss the next stage or any upcoming stage for that matter. Team Management supplied us with very detailed stage notes for every single stage. Details like junctions – elevations – road surfaces – landmarks – dangers – distance – hotel locations and a map of the particular stage every day. Apart from a quick glance we didn't really spend too much time researching. Some of the others soaked up every detail but I was concerned this may have a negative effect, causing more anxiety and fear of what lay ahead. John and myself opt to register the important stuff and generally just get on with it. Whatever we have to face on this mega challenge we will deal with it in due course. Two hugely important members of our support crew are Seán Brennan and his friend Brian Buirds. They head off before everyone each morning and have the difficult task of route signage and management. The lads place arrows and signage at each junction and turn for the cyclists and the support crew vehicles. This job can be a nightmare in some busy areas with many roads and junctions, but hugely important to the peloton of cyclists to navigate our way and stay on the correct route.

STAGE 6   Show Low AZ - Springville AZ   58 miles
Tuesday October 19th, 2000.

A DAY TO FORGET - The shortest stage, for what was planned as an easy stage, it turned out to be a shit day. Teams had a late depart at 10am and 10.45am respectively due to the shorter stage. Very heavy rain from the start which became torrential and cold for all of the 3.5 hours we spent on the bike! The roads were undulating with many sharp hills with fast descents. I had a speed wobble as I hurled down one such descent. For those who have never had the experience of a speed wobble on a descent at high speed, it is frightening. The bike takes on a life of its own. It starts as a small wobble and quickly becomes much more. The handlebars are shaking violently from side to side and you're doing all you can to stay upright. Terrified of crashing, you try to slow down as quickly as you can and pull over to the side of the road. It's one of the most terrifying things you can experience on a bike. It also occurs in motorbikes and skateboards. It starts in road bikes when something causes the front wheel to accelerate to one side. A bump in the road surface, a gust of wind, a faulty wheel or a rider sneezing or shivering with the cold, as in my case. The best way to control it is to try and change your weight distribution or clamp your legs onto the top tube or cross bar and use the back break to slow down and stop, or until it goes away. I had experienced a speed wobble before this but not at high speed. This time it was frightening and made me nervous as I tried to continue on. Seán Kelly had seen it many times in the pro peloton. As we pedalled along at pace on the flat in the pouring rain, Seán positioned himself really close to me and then began to hit my right buttock and thigh with his handlebars and brake lever. He wanted me to concentrate and take my mind away from the fright I had on the earlier descent. It worked. Seán of course knew what he was doing. His actions were causing me to react and pedal clear and concentrate myself again on the job in hand. I began to warm up and put the earlier wobble out of my head. Today we had one food stop at 35 miles in a wooded area. Cyclists were frozen, saturated and generally in bad form. I went straight to Mick Cowell at the food truck. Margaret and himself had soup and sambos to warm people up. I asked him had he any cognac. Mick did not disappoint and presented me with a big tumbler of Hennessy Brandy. It hit the spot for me. I finished the rest of the stage with Kelly regaling tales of cyclists who he saw having speed wobbles and crashing out of races. It was a very scenic route along mountain plateaus, with pine forests, a typical alpine stage with 9,000ft of climbing. Tonight we are staying at the Rode Inn in Springerville, AZ

Today was a difficult day, it took a lot out of the groups, it was good to finish and get into the hotel in the early afternoon. More time to rest, recover and recuperate.

STAGE 7 = Springerville AZ - Socorro NM 157 miles
Wednesday October 11th, 2000.

A beast of a stage and the longest of the USA Coast to Coast cycle challenge. Group 1 departed after breakfast at 6am. Group 2 at 6.45am and now reduced to eight cyclists. The fact our group 2 now consists of only eight riders is becoming very important, and this is why. Riding in a bunch means that only the riders in the front "break" the wind providing shelter to those behind. When riding at the front your heart rate is typically around twenty beats higher than in the middle or at the back. So doing a stint on the front and then rotating towards the back is important for recovery before making your way to the front again. Two riders normally cycle side by side, in our case now with eight riders we had a formation of two lines containing four riders constantly rotating in sequence. While doing your turn on the front and sheltering those behind, you are also responsible for keeping the pace at a certain speed and pointing out hazards. Depending on wind and weather and road conditions different average speeds are applied. At times it can be necessary to ride in single file or in echelon formation (think fighter planes) to try and cut through a strong side wind. The average speed, the formation and amount of time to spend on the front during each turn is always discussed and changed as required during the day's stage. The fact our peloton in group 2 is now reduced to eight riders has its pros and cons. We are all very strong riders in peak condition and working very well as a unit, we understand and support each other completely. However, with only eight, each one of us must spend more time in the front, in the wind, at higher heart rate every day expending more energy with less recovery time drafting or slipstreaming in the bunch. This basically means we have much higher fatigue loads to deal with on a daily basis. The masseurs have said that they have to work much harder on the members of our group each evening to clear knots and flush out the lactate, due to the extra stress on our bodies every day. We crossed into New Mexico on today's stage and for seven of the eight hours and seven minutes we spent on the bikes, it rained. Heavy rain nearly all day. New Mexico got one third of its annual rain fall in those seven hours!! Some cyclists did not start this morning, a mixture of injuries, fatigue and being pissed off. We lose an hour today as we cross the State Border. This super long stage is all rolling hills on straight stretches. Terrain is ever changing, pine forests to desert rock. A hard day in desperate conditions. News reaches us before we finish that there has been a couple of crashes concerning group 1. Descents today are treacherous in the rain. Phil Lavery had come down heavy at a railway crossing and required stitches, (on returning home after completing the challenge he discovered that he had fractured his hip) others were unable to finish the stage. Some very tired bodies at the dinner table tonight. Sé Weston who started the trip in our group developed a niggly knee injury over a few days, he moved to group 1 to give himself a chance to heal.

However, after meeting with the Management and Team Leaders this evening, it was decided that Sé had lost his battle to the injury and would be flying home the next day. This had a big effect on our group. Sé was a hugely experienced cyclist and a massive addition to the team. He was now heading home. We all wondered who would be next?

Every night after dinner a team briefing took place, going through that days stage and the next one, pinpointing the important stuff and any issues to be dealt with. Eamón Duffy was the director of fundraising at the NCBI and the Blazing Saddles main man. Eamón is a larger than life figure and was the chief organiser of this challenge, having driven and planned the entire route and booked the accommodation the previous year. The NCBI provides services to over 8,000 people annually who have significant sight loss. It is the agency responsible for the delivery of all services to visually impaired people in this country. Eamón launched Blazing Saddles in 1991, picking up the name from the Mel Brooks film. The Blazing Saddles have been phenomenally successful and raised millions of euros and visited many countries. Eamón is also a brilliant motivator and always makes the impossible seem very doable. His speeches every night were always colourful and full of grit and determination.

STAGE 8   =   Socorro NM - Ruidoso NM   114 miles
Thursday October 12th, 2000.

Group 1 departed at 6.45am and Group 2 at 7.30am. Guess what? It was raining again for the first 35miles! This type of event really tests your mental strength and mindset.

As we rolled away from the Hotel this morning it was very poignant to see Sé Weston putting his bags and bike in one of the support vehicles to head for the nearest airport and his flight home. One of our compatriots was gone from the bunch. This challenge had claimed its first victim! We had to get on with the job in hand. First food stop today was at 46 miles. I thought we'd never get there. We were sluggish for the first few hours after the big effort of the previous day. The legs felt really heavy and slow to get going. Things improved after the food stop and we rolled along with purpose finishing with two big climbs, the Nogal and Rio Bonito, before reaching our hotel for the night – Holiday Inn Express. Tonight we ate down the road at the Lee Cattle Restaurant where the meat is scrumptious. Today's cycling time 6hrs 55 mins. Average speed 16.8 mph.

STAGE 9   =   Ruidoso NM - Roswell NM 101 miles
Friday October 13th, 2000.

Group 1 depart at 10am. Group 2 at 10.45am

Ah lads, this was badly needed................ A beautiful stage - sunshine – flat roads – good surfaces – a tailwind – A Cyclists dream. Especially after the previous few exceptionally hard stages. The mood in our group is really good today. We have one food stop at 38 miles.

After that we encounter two climbs and celebrate getting over the last of the Rocky Mountains, we opt to go in single file as the road is narrow and the surface is really good. I suffer a rear tyre blow out at 45 mph. I don't know how I managed to hold the bike and stay upright. A quick wheel change and away again. Our mechanic John Keegan said we resembled a team doing a time trial in the Tour de France. We race along and eat up the miles to the Ramada Inn in Roswell NM.

Average speed 26 mph. New Mexico is a South Eastern State with a very scenic and diverse landscape including desert and mountains. It's influenced by both Hispanic and Native American culture. There are only about twelve people per square mile. There are more sheep and cattle in the state than people. Famous people born in NM, singer/ songwriter John Denver and actress Demi Moore were both born here in Roswell.

STAGE 10 = Roswell NM - Brownfield TX 141 miles
Saturday October 14th, 2000.

At breakfast this morning, things get heated. The food provided is not good to say the least, my motto – "get it into ya, you are going to need it later". Not everyone thinks the same. Not everyone under supreme psychological and physical pressure reacts the same (one of my strongest characteristics luckily). Tempers are high and flaring and patience is wearing thin.

Just another day on this tough endurance event!!

Group 1 depart at 6.45am Group 2 @at 7.30am

After 92 miles of today's stage we cross the Texas State Line. We are on Rt. 380 for 139miles. The road is practically straight the whole way. Denis Twomey from Cork is the pilot of the tandem carrying Joe Bollard. Joe being visually impaired jokes that he could sit on the front of the tandem as the road is so straight! As we roll on, we start to monitor the length of time we can see big trucks on the road ahead after they overtake us. The roads are so long and straight you can see the back of the last truck that went past fifteen minutes later. We get our first introduction to Oil Fields and the very distinctive smell emanating from them. Later in the day we came across the Cotton Plantations. Our group are working well and we eat up the miles. We pull into the Crystal Palace Inn after 6hrs and 50 minutes on the bike.

Average speed for today 20.6 mph. I was the last to get massage this evening. Later, as I enter the El Palacio Mexican restaurant for dinner next door to our hotel the guys shout at me to look up at the wall behind me. The Blazing Saddles Management have put a map of the USA on the wall and coloured in black what we had cycled so far, and with a lighter grey line on what was left to complete. It really threw me. I had struggled a fair bit mentally during the day with doubt and suffering and pain in general. One of my hardest days so far. I said to myself. "Feck it we have ten stages done and dusted but look at what still lays ahead, this is a monster". I had to correct myself and remind myself to just take it one stage and one day at a time. Like eating an elephant. Small bites.

STAGE 11 = Brownfield TX - Aspermont TX 130 miles
Sunday October 15th, 2000.

Group 1 depart at 6.45am Group 2 at 7.30am. We're on US Highway Rt. 380 again today. This East – West Highway is 673 miles wide and we stay on it all the way across the State of Texas! Very flat stage today with extensive farming carried out all along the route. Weather is nice and the mood in the peloton is good. Food stops at 53miles and 105miles.

Our motel is the Hickmans Motel – I won't be going back!! No place to safely store our bikes overnight so we must bring them to our rooms. John and myself found this a pain in the butt and came up with a plan. When you wake up during the night as you twist or turn, or go to the loo, the last thing you want to see looking at you is your bike. So anytime we had to have bikes in the room they went under the bed or flat on the floor out of eye shot. It's the small things!!

Cycling time today 6hrs 10 mins – Average speed 20.8 mph. I fitted two new tyres this evening. I had got a number of punctures and covered 1,250 miles on the first set.

Many of the rooms in the Hickman Motel were infested with cockroaches. In the showers, everyplace. We came up with a plan. We put a bedside lamp just inside the front door of the room, they made for the light. We had a great sleep that night. Most of the others hardly slept a wink!

STAGE 12 = Aspermont TX - Jacksboro TX 136 miles
Monday October 16th, 2000.

Departs at 6.45am for Group 1 and 7.30am for Group 2.

The eight of us making up Group 2 were cycling very strongly as a unit, we had become really comfortable with each other and we worked like a pro team. You get to know peoples riding styles and characteristics, how they climb and descend. How they get out of the saddle or lean into a corner. Jim Tuohy – Michael Gallen – Gerard O'Donoghue – Liam Mc Convey (Teak) – James O Donnell – Martin Kearney – John Mannion – Myself. James was the youngest rider on the whole trip. At twenty one year's of age, this was a brilliant experience for him and a credit to himself and his family to have raised the sponsorship funds for the trip. His youthful enthusiasm and general tom foolery was a tonic every day for our group. Jim Tuohy was the voice of reason, commanding but always with a trickle of fun. Michael Gallen and Martin Kearney were super strong and always willing to do more than their share of work especially on the longest stages. Teak as the nick name suggests was tough and brought a bit of an edge to the group, regularly putting us in our place and firmly believing he was the toughest cyclist in our bunch! John Mannion was getting stronger and stronger every day and his attitude and recovery was inspirational. We're like a close family as we knock out the miles each day. We are not a team because we cycle together. We are a team because we respect, trust, and care for each other. Today's scenery was like the weather, dull and boring, fairly dark and overcast and grey, but no rain thankfully. Cycling time for the stage 6hrs.31mins. Average speed 20.6mph. Tonight we are in the Jacksboro Inn with dinner served at the Village Kitchen next door.

STAGE 13 = Jacksboro TX - Greenville TX 152 miles
Tuesday October 17th, 2000.

Group 1 depart at 6.45am Group 2 at 7.30am

We started this morning on very busy roads, plenty of big articulated trucks and heavy traffic, as we are just North of Fort Worth. The first two hours were stressful trying to navigate our way through such heavy traffic. The weather brightened up as the day went on, and so did our demeanour, as we went through some nice small towns like Bridgeport, Gainesville, Slidell, Celina, Blueridge and Farmersville. After the food stop at 50 miles

Group 1 had a crash. Someone touched a wheel in front and it brought down a few more. The RTE Sport personality Tracey Piggot had to be brought to hospital with a suspected hand fracture and some others had cuts and bruises.

After the second food stop at 106 miles as we entered the outskirts of Greenville the traffic again became very heavy. A police escort was provided for us to guide us safely to the Best Western Hotel with dinner at the Kettle Restaurant next door.

The police who escort us were on push bikes and came to the outskirts of town to lead us in. After a mile behind them moving at a really slow pace, we decided to just push them the last four miles to the hotel!! Lovely guys with a great welcome for us.

Cycling time 7hrs 55 mins. Average 20 mph

STAGE 14 = Greenville TX - Texarkana AR 144 miles
Wednesday October 18th, 2000.

Group 1 depart at 7am. Group 2 at 7.45am

We get out of the busy Greenville traffic with the aid of a police escort in police cars this time and settle into a nice rhythm on lovely rolling country roads with nice surfaces. Our second food stop today is a milestone and we have a little celebration, we have passed the halfway mark of the challenge. Mood in the group in the afternoon is good and really positive and a feeling that we have achieved something by getting to the halfway mark. The sun even made an appearance for the afternoon. We got to the Best Western Hotel after 7hrs and 21mins on the bike, average speed 19.8 mph. We entered the state of Arizona at the very end of today's stage leaving Texas behind. Dinner tonight is at La Carate, a Mexican Restaurant 1.5miles from the hotel. I'm on laundry duty this evening. It's a real pain at times, as we were given three team issue Blazing Saddles jerseys, two short sleeved and one long sleeved. Keeping them washed and dried is not easy. Some hotels have no washing facilities and when we get in late after the longer stages it's hard to make time to get everything done. This evening is an exception, I march off to "The Soap Opera" excellent laundry near the hotel with a bag of my own and John Mannion's and return later with everything in pristine shape. La Carate has a nice bar and we have a few beers after dinner and appreciate again having passed the half way stage.

STAGE 15 = Texarkana AR - Camden AR   83 miles
Thursday October 19th, 2000.

Group 1 depart at 10am Group 2 at 10.45am

The later start was due to the shorter stage and to give us extra recovery and rest. You don't really sleep any later than usual but it's a bit of extra time being horizontal, which means resting.

I had to do my media duties and therefore was up early to do a radio interview. I did my interviews in Irish (Gaeilge) and John Mannion my roommate had an arrangement with Galway Bay FM radio where he gave interviews in English. James O Donnell in our group said his mother was listening to both our interviews as she was a fluent Irish speaker. She asked James "Are John and Máirtín doing the same cycle? As they seem to recount the stages differently!" After my first radio chat where I told the truth, having cramped badly and barely made it to the finish, everyone at home was really worried about me. So, I tended to not dramatise things and even make it sound a lot better than it actually was. While John said exactly how hard the stages were and how he and others were feeling, so it sounded like we were on a different cycle. This stage was nice and we ended up on quiet and beautiful country roads away from traffic. The road surface for the first 14 miles was very rough and caused a few punctures but improved immensely after that. A beautiful tree lined route with just a few rolling hills. At 33 miles we enter the town of Hope, the birthplace of Bill Clinton. Nice relaxed atmosphere in the group as we enjoyed the countryside and the shorter stage. We got to the Ramada Inn in Camden AR after 4hrs and 30mins at an average of 19.8 mph.

After getting a massage and having returned to my room I noticed I had left my t-shirt in the medical room. I popped back down later to get it and got a bit of a shock. Caitríona Devilly our team nurse (also a Galwegian) was treating quite a lot of cyclists for saddle sores. I had not realised so many were suffering with the problem. Earlier in the year during a training event I was cycling with Brian Connaughton, a keen cyclist who had won the Rás (multi day stage race in Ireland). We had a discussion about shaving the legs. Brian advised me to shave everywhere. "What do you mean"? I said. "The sack and all around that area," he said, "You are going to be sitting in that saddle for 3,000 miles and that is a lot of friction and sweat". I took Brian's very solid advice and thankfully did not suffer with saddle sores. The main reason cyclists shave their legs is that it makes treating cuts and road rash easier, bandages and plasters can be applied more easily with less chance of infection. It also makes massage more comfortable.

STAGE 16 = Camden AR - Pine Bluff AR 82 miles
Friday October 20th,2000.

Group 1 depart at 10am Group 2 at 10.15am

Another lovely stage today, on country back roads. In group 2 we decide to ride at a fairly strong pace to the food stop at 50miles and afterwards to the finish. The quicker we get off the bikes the sooner our recovery starts. Seán Kelly joins us for the run in to the Best Western Hotel. We cover the 82 miles in just under 4 hrs. A lovely stage. Massage, rest, recovery, rehydration and recuperation are so important on a gruelling event like this and cannot be overstated.

We are putting out big power every day, burning in excess of 10,000 calories most days in all kinds of weather conditions. Then we have all the off-bike duties to attend to. Bike maintenance and cleaning, laundry, food, packing and unpacking. The body is under constant stress unless it's horizontal. So we try to make sure to lay down with the legs elevated as much as possible. I washed my bike this evening and after a conversation with John Keegan one of our mechanics I opted to replace the chain. I had cycled over 1,850 miles on the other one so far on this trip and the gear changing was not as smooth as I would have liked in the last day or two. John checked the chain and confirmed that it had stretched a good bit and needed to be changed.

STAGE 17 = Pine Bluff AR - Lula MS 132 miles
Saturday October 21st, 2000.

Group 1 depart at 7am Group 2 at 7.45am

The contour for today is mainly flat, after a cool morning the day brightens up. We cross the Arkansas River and enter the State of Mississippi, crossing over the Mississippi River in the afternoon. Beautiful countryside with wooded areas and gentle flowing roads. I have developed a bit of tendonitis in my feet. The soles of my feet are very sore and I feel as if I'm being stabbed with a knife at times. At the food stops I submerge them in ice to reverse the pain, which works for about 20 miles and then it starts again.

At best it's uncomfortable at worst its excruciating. The masseurs do their best to relieve the tension in my feet and I up the ice treatment. I try not to focus on it as the more you do the bigger the problem becomes. Lady Luck Casino Motel for the night. It was all over the place very spread out and noisy with hundreds of slot machines and gaming machines. Not on my list to return to!

6 hrs 38 mins on the bike, average speed today 20 mph.

STAGE 18 = Lula MS - Tupelo MS   139 miles
Sunday October 22nd, 2000.

Group 1 depart at 7am. Group 2 at 7.45am – Food stops at 54 miles and 105 miles.

Mississippi is a beautiful state to cycle through. The stage is mostly flat with lovely rolling country roads. I'm in agony with my feet in the afternoon. It's decided at the second food stop that both groups cycle home together. We get into the Ramada Inn after 7 hrs 11 mins. of cycling, average speed 18.8 mph. We are in Tupelo this evening, the birthplace of Elvis Presley. We decide to go and visit the tiny bungalow where he was born and the museum that has been added at the back. They don't serve beer in Tupelo on Sunday, however we had a police escort to the hotel earlier and one of the cops was of Irish descent. Of course, he obliged the few of us who valued a couple of bottles and he returned with some stocks for us which was really appreciated. Those few beers every night helped six or eight of us relax and forget about the stresses we were dealing with daily and put us off to sleep every night. Good quality sleep is critical, allowing the heart to rest and the cells and tissues to repair. This helps the body recover especially after extreme physical exertion.

STAGE 19 = Tupelo MS - Lawrenceburg TN   140 miles
Monday October 23rd, 2000.

Group 1 depart at 7am Group 2 at 7.45am

After a pretty cool start the temperatures ramped up to 90 degrees Fahrenheit. We spent most of the stage in Natchez Trace Parkway for 112 miles. It's a recreational road and scenic drive that actually goes through three states, Mississippi, Alabama and Tennessee. The Tennessee River and Bridge is spectacular. The Natchez Trace is a designated bicycle route and the road surface is good with many rolling hills to contend with and 4,500 ft of climbing.

Best Western Hotel is our stop for tonight. – Cycling time today 6.30 mins. average speed 20 mph.

Dinner and breakfast is at Shoney's across the road.

Every day is a new battle, finding the mental strength to push through the difficulties, to have the correct mindset to know that no matter how hard the situation is, it will change, to believe in yourself and to push on, to be smart yet strong. To be able to push when required and conserve to save energy. Small pains and discomforts as you start in the morning when you clip into your pedals facing a hundred mile plus stage, becomes a very big issue very quickly, if you let it. The weather conditions and type of terrain also play a part on your mood and how you feel. Mr. Doubt and Mr. Suffer are sitting on my shoulders everyday making themselves heard. I acknowledge them but I will not give in to them. I push on with the rest of our group, everyone is suffering and hurting to some degree. "Misery is a choice".

STAGE 20 = Lawrenceburg TN - Winchester TN   95 miles
Tuesday October 24th, 2000.

Media Duty – Radio Interview at 6.30am. Would rather have rested for another hour!

Group 1 depart at 8am. Group 2 at 8.45am. For the first 50 miles of today, we cycle through the Amish Community homes and farming area. There are about 250 farm families who choose not to have electricity, telephones, computers, cars or indoor plumbing. Most of the Amish families have ten or more children, sometimes up to twenty. They make their own clothing and go barefoot during the warm months. The three main crops on the Amish farms are tobacco, corn and sorghum cane. We passed many of their black horse drawn buggies along our route today. The Amish are devout Christians. We get into our Best Western Hotel in Winchester after 4hrs 40 mins. average speed 20.5 mph.

I opt to change my tyres again and fit two new Continental 25mm Gator Skins for the last few stages. I also fit new brake blocks, the existing ones are fairly well worn and we have some very fast and dangerous descents tomorrow. Five stages to go now.

STAGE 21 = Winchester TN - Calhoun GA   118 miles
Wednesday October 25th, 2000.

Group 1 depart at 6.45am   Group 2 at 7.30am   6,600 ft of climbing.

In and out of three states again today. Tennessee, Alabama and Georgia. Described by the Team Management as an exceptional ride, really beautiful and the most difficult of all, frightening downhills with very acute hair-pin bends. Very long climbs today that go on for six to eight miles and plenty of them. We were in the Smokey Mountains and the Appalachian Mountains later in the day. Strict 20 mph speed restrictions on the downhills as they are so dangerous. At 54 miles we cross the Georgia State Border, we lose another hour. Ireland is 5 hours ahead now. After many more climbs we get to the Super 8 Motel in Calhoun.

Cycling time 6 hrs 30 mins, average speed 18.2 mph. Dinner and breakfast served at the Chuck Wagon Restaurant beside the hotel.

STAGE 22 = Calhoun GA - Gainesville GA   90 miles
Thursday October 26th, 2000.

Group 1 depart at 7.am   Group 2 at 7.45 am - climbing over 6,000 ft. today.

The notes for today's stage say "Plenty of Climbing – Tough Day".

We start the day in foggy conditions causing a bit of a chill, especially on the descents. We nip along at a good pace up and down all day. Eventful day for the support crew, one of the RV vehicles breaks down and has to be taken away for repairs. News also filters through to us about a hotel change. The planned hotel for tonight had been hit by a tornado two days earlier!

We rock into Gainesville after 4hrs 46mins on the bike, average 18.6mph.

New Hotel is a Best Western, a hotel with only 'best' in the name. It's laundry duty for me this evening.

Dinner is at China King Restaurant about a mile down the road.

STAGE 23 = Gainesville GA - Greenwood SC 124 miles
Friday October 27th,2000.

Group 1 depart at 7am. Group 2 at 7.45am. As we begin the stage I can smell the change in the air. I can smell the salt in the atmosphere, the sea air is getting closer and it's a very welcome signal. 352 miles to the Atlantic, to

59

stay upright and stay healthy to the end. I felt the mixture of appreciation, apprehension and emotion course through my veins. Feelings of fear, exhilaration, and passion. "Control your thoughts and adjust your mindset, stay focused. You have to finish the elephant bit by bit I said to myself."

After 75 miles today we cross the Savannah River and enter South Carolina state line. This is our tenth and final state.Yippee!! It turned out to be a beautiful day with nice roads and scenery. I really enjoyed the run in, the last 30 miles after the food stop to the Ramada Inn in Greenwood. Cycling time 6 hrs 11 mins. average speed 20 mph.

Everyone has a pep in their step at dinner tonight. The dream is almost a reality.

STAGE 24 = Greenwood SC - Orangeburg SC   120 miles
Saturday 24th October,2000.

The semi-final if you like. The second last stage. 228 miles to the finish line in Charleston SC. The sun was out early for us as we got down to business. I was still in a lot of pain with the Tendonitis in my feet. I also had pain shooting up my left leg for the last few days. The ice treatment only worked for short periods. I seem to suffer more in the heat. I decided two days ago to introduce a few Difene tablets to my diet! Difene is a painkilling medicine which reduces inflammation and swelling, basically to relieve pain and inflammation. I did not want to overdo them as they can cause constipation among other side effects and can be severe on the stomach, and I don't take medication for anything because I normally don't suffer from anything! This tendonitis was not going away and the pain was excruciating. The only way to keep it at bay was taking a few Difene. I tended to wait until the first food stop of the day and take one then to help get me through the rest of the stage. I was not going to fail at this juncture. We hit a stiff headwind for most of the day, climbing was 2,200 ft in total. The tandem and two more cyclists from Group 1 joined us for the last 40 miles after the second food stop. It was nice to chat to a few different faces as we headed for Orangeburg SC.

Hotel for tonight is the Holiday Inn, a nice spot that serves dinner and breakfast. We have many more join us tonight for a beer, the mood is celebratory and relief all in one. We still have over 108 miles to go.

STAGE 25 – THE FINAL STAGE = Orangeburg SC - Charleston SC 108 miles Sunday October 29th, 2000.

All groups head off together this morning. A real carnival atmosphere. The pace is really slow though and boring to the food stop at 50 miles. After that we are allowed ride faster for the next 30 miles, stopping to re-group again and all cycle to the finish line at the Charleston on the Beach Hotel and the Atlantic Ocean. The four cyclists from Galway who rode in Group 2 were given the honour to lead the whole team for the last ten miles. It was such a pleasure to look back occasionally from the front and see a line of green jerseys coming behind us. Most cyclists just cycled straight down the beach and into the Atlantic.

What a great feeling and sense of achievement. Finished and did not miss one mile of the 3,000 miles. Summary of how I had felt during the epic journey as follows...

I felt good, I felt pain, I felt sore, I felt depressed, lonely, elated, content, pissed off and annoyed with some cyclists, and close to others during this challenge across America.

I also felt apprehensive and nervous some days, but mostly determined, focused and totally concentrated. My mindset was mostly strong all through under all kinds of pressure. The notes for today said "After the ceremonial dipping of the wheels, well done, you've made it. It is an achievement that you will treasure for a lifetime and your children will treasure it and their children because you achieved something really great and unique. Not many people have done it. Celebrate your achievement, riders and support crew you have done it. It was a team effort".

Blazing Saddles USA COAST to COAST Cycle Challenge for the NCBI

3,000 miles x 25 days - October 2000.

For the record, while cycling across the USA I got 13 punctures, changed front and back tyres twice, replaced a set of brake blocks and also replaced my chain.

THE TEAM
Cyclists – Support Crew – Mechanics – Medical – Camera Crews

Ann Acheson - Kildare	Alfie Acheson - Kildare
Joe Bollard – Wicklow	Gerry Beggs - Down
Niamh Bonnar – Dublin	Margaret Cowell - Dublin
Denis Broderick – Derry	Mick Cowell - Kildare
Peter Bryson – Derry	Ray de Brun - Galway
Paul Butler – Meath	Christine O Connor - Galway
Vincent Crowley – Dublin	Caitriona Devilly - Dublin
Pat Cummins – Limerick	Eamon Duffy - Louth
Michael Gallen – Tyrone	John Falconer - Dublin
Alan Geoghan – Offaly	John Keegan - Dublin
Martin Kearney – Galway	Bridie O Neill - Wicklow
Pete Kelly -Galway	John O Neill - Dublin
John Mannion – Galway	Vincent Power - Tipperary
James O Donnell – Galway	John Perry - Dublin
Máirtín Óg Mc Donagh - Galway	
Seán Kelly – Tipperary	Sean Brennan - San Diego
Phil Lavery – Waterford	Brian Buirds - San Diego
Fergal Lee – Kildare	Paul Malone - Dublin
Brendan Mc Auliffe – Offaly	Liam (Teak) Mc Convey - Down
Seamus Mc Elroy – Monaghan	Eugene O Connor - Laois
Gerard O Donoghue – Kerry	Barry O Halloran - Dublin
Tracy Piggot – Kildare	Adrian Rafferty **RIP** - Down
Declan Sugrue – Dublin	Denis Toomey - Cork
Jim Tuohy – Tipperary	Sé Weston - Dublin

Chapter 5

IT HIT ME HARD AND LINGERED LONG

It started to go wrong with devastating consequences all around me!!

"Everyone has a plan until they get punched in the mouth" – Mike Tyson.

That was Tyson's famous reply to a reporter when asked whether he was worried about Evander Holyfield and his fight plan. I took up boxing while in my teens for a couple of years. I learned about self-defence, speed and resistance and the importance of preparation. Fights are won by doing the hard work in the gym for months and months. This is where you lay the foundation for the challenges ahead. Same applies to life. Holyfield won that fight against all the odds. He did get punched in the mouth many times. However he adapted his original plan to deal with 'right now reality' therein lies the message.

When you are running a business, any business, as it starts to grow and expand the demands on the owners/proprietors begin to also ramp up. Increasing turnover brings with it a load of extra work and stress. More clients and customers necessitate more staff and more expansion. All through the nineties and into the noughties my plant truck and machinery business was steadily growing and gaining traction. I knew the business well and was extremely confident in what we were doing. The next natural progression was to take on bigger contract work, including site-works, pipe-laying, kerbing, concrete works along with bulk excavation, rock breaking and supplying stone and material. I also began to see other opportunities around the construction and development arena.

I started off by purchasing a couple of properties from O'Malley Construction. Deposits were off set in lieu of work completed on sites, while acquiring a mortgage for the balance. It was a perfect easy way to purchase a property. We were working on a couple of different sites and meeting the deposit requirement in this manner was painless and very doable. I was now moving in different circles, coming in contact with entrepreneurs and developers, bankers and movers and shakers.

The Huntsman Inn on College Road on the East side of Galway City, overlooking the shores of Lough Atalia, about 10 minutes' walk from Eyre Square is where a lot of wheeling and dealing was being done. No one was talking in hundreds of thousands, it began with millions and then...... well let's say it went mad. The Huntsman is a boutique hotel, a popular bar and restaurant and has spacious car parking and well landscaped lawns and planting. The selection of cars and 4x4's on show some days resembled a stroll down the port of Marbella. The vast green lawns were often used for landing the helicopters! (as you do) was where I closed a few deals here myself. Property and land deals were not the exception, I shook hands on machinery and truck deals and finalised the paperwork and finance agreements in the one spot. I'd often agree a deal with a machinery distributor for a couple of diggers at a table over breakfast, the finance representative was then summoned, rates were thrashed out and agreed and the paperwork was signed up. All this while enjoying your poached eggs and bacon! It was like Wall Street. Bankers from all the main banks, solicitors and accountants regularly made appearances advising clients and closing deals. At times clinching a deal meant celebratory drinks or a full session. Discussions only momentarily disturbed by the distinctive hum of a high-powered vehicle arriving or leaving the car park. This was life during those years in the early to mid 00's and I was bang in the middle of it with my own little monopoly portfolio! I started to identify bigger opportunities and get into the game much deeper if you like. The deals began running into millions. I was now a player. I had an interest in anything that went up for sale in the locality and I was even trying to negotiate stuff that was not for sale in the background, particularly if it fitted in with some plot or property I had already acquired. The early deals went well. Houses and a couple of acres were purchased and flipped again for a nice profit, which was then re-invested in bigger deals. I then decided to go the full hog and actually develop our own sites. Applying for planning permission for complete projects, including shop units, offices and housing. We could do the groundworks and site preparation ourselves for my development company with the plant and machinery company and supply stone and fill from our quarries. One of my businesses would work directly for the other, which meant keeping control of costs and quality and generating profits within my own ventures. Ideal I hear you say!

It Hit Me Hard and Lingered On

As I alluded to earlier, with growth and expansion comes pressure and stress and a whole pile of management and organisational responsibilities. Turnover had now more than quadrupled, the original plant truck and machinery company and quarries were in a good solid place and in good shape. Most of the plant was paid for and still in good nick, as I always prided myself on keeping stuff well maintained. The development company was only set up at the end of 2005 early 2006 and had heavy borrowings, solely based on acquiring land and property purchased at the current market values. The projects in the pipeline most of which were in the planning process were feasible and would be very profitable according to all the costing and estimations. The full-time employee numbers were growing rapidly now with many sub-contractors also employed on an on- going basis. At the top level however, we were creaking. I was trying to handle all of the day to day stuff myself. This was now a substantial amount of work. I was flat to the mat every day. Site visits and site meetings, organising plant and trucks, supply of stone and material. Keeping on top of fuel deliveries for all sites, dealing with employees and customers and clients. Attending planning meetings and project meetings with architects and engineers, banks and finance houses, accountants and solicitors. I was never off the phone or off the road. My jeep was my mobile office. Family time was almost non-existent. I needed all the hours I could get to try and squeeze the most out of each day. My brain was constantly engaged, I was operating at peak performance. Exercise and particularly cycling was squeezed in whenever I got a chance, once or twice during the week and on Saturday or Sunday. I was socialising a good bit every weekend, it was like hitting a relief valve. I could release myself from the constant busyness and relax with a few beers. The buzz of my life was amazing and I was really enjoying it. Máirtín Óg Plant and Machinery was involved in different projects in Connemara and Galway City. Foundation works for private individuals for one off houses and small projects for local builders. Supplying stone from the quarry to various local jobs big and small, notable contracts like the runway and terminal for Aer Arann at Inverin. Site-works at Radio na Gaeltachta and TG4, local road jobs for Galway County Council. Around the city we were involved in bigger housing schemes or doing bulk excavation for landmark developments like the Galway Bay Hotel, Jury's Hotel, The Eyre Square Centre and so on. Road projects such as the Oranmore by-pass and the demolition of the Rahoon Flats. It was fantastic to be involved in this progressive work and to have the opportunity to play a very active part in the progress of many different schemes.

Óg Developments (the development company) had secured planning permission for a mixed-use development in the middle of the town in Carraroe after a fraught and prolonged process. Getting planning permission in the Connemara Gaeltacht is extremely difficult for one-off housing. You must first demonstrate a housing need and that you are working in the area or adding to the local economy, that you are living in the area and that you can speak Irish. The Planning Board and Galway County Council came up with a strategy of getting people to live in villages where most services already existed, sewage schemes, electricity supply and water, transport, close proximity to schools, shops, pubs, restaurants, public transport etc. The other side of this was a consideration to cutting back on the sporadic one-off houses popping up all over the place in such a 'high scenic amenity area'.

My scheme ticked all these boxes. This was very far from plain sailing however. Ironing out the design and bulk issues between the architects and the planners took time, add to this some local objections and then last but by no means least the Irish language and heritage protection groups. After having meetings after meetings with all the various groups and without splitting hairs here I eventually secured planning permission with some pretty hefty conditions. Big contributions for development fees to Galway County Council, and a bond insurance payment before starting works. The number of house units was reduced from twenty four to twenty, to increase green area space, which I had no problem with. I had to sell eighteen of the houses to Irish speakers from the area and the scheme including the shop units and offices could not be connected to the Carraroe main sewage scheme until it was up graded. While this upgrading project was in the pipeline no one seemed to know when it would start. I had another development with An Bord Pleanála (Planning Board) awaiting a decision. So, while waiting for green lights on these developments was painful, both financially and personally I had no choice. Dealing with all these additional issues was taking up a lot of time and adding considerably to my stress levels. Rightly or wrongly, I opted to always shield my family from business issues as much as possible, especially the problematic stuff. Looking back at it now, I know I should have taken on some senior staff, people to help share the load at an organisational and managerial level. I needed top professional advice at close quarters from a financial and tax efficient perspective which I didn't have at the time. I had engaged separate accountants and tax advisers for both companies, but they operated at arm's length which was not suitable to my scenario. 'The monster' meaning my business portfolio and interests had grown hugely over the last few years and I was still trying to cope without making the necessary adjustments in line with the expansion and growth. Invoicing clients was slow and began to get slower as I was not spending enough time in the office dealing with the paperwork side of the businesses. I physically could not make the time. This was a costly mistake. The next even bigger financial bobo, (on the advice of a bank manager) I moved all my banking business into one bank, to negotiate a better rate I was told. That essentially meant all truck and machinery and investment finance from the plant company (Máirtín Óg Plant and Machinery) and all development and investment finance for Óg Developments and existing loans with other banks were all settled and paid off and replaced with a new financial arrangement under one umbrella with AIB. My mother always said "Never put all your eggs in the one hanky" – Oh mother why didn't I listen!

Great news. Finally in February 2006 we got the go ahead for the mixed-use (housing, offices and shop units) project in the village. The Carraroe sewage improvement scheme had also got the green light shortly after that. I actually had machinery working on it for Coffey Construction. So, all guns blazing. The mixed-use development was split in two. One site consisted of the twenty houses and a commercial building to the front with four/five units/offices. The second site consisted of a large commercial building including three ground floor units, one of which had planning as a medical centre and two overhead offices and car parking for forty cars. Both sites were in the centre of the village 250 metres apart. The project was valued at €8.6 million. AIB had committed to finance the whole development initially and crucially releasing funding for the housing site including the units/offices. When builders tendered for the project in its entirety the actual tender was split into two. A quote for the housing site and another for the medical centre site. My own plant and machinery company (Máirtín Óg Plant) got stuck into the excavation and stone filling for both sites as well as the pipe laying, kerb laying footpaths and landscaping. The builders took over at raft level. In the space of eight months the site works had progressed at a fast pace and we were working well alongside the builders. The housing site and medical centre site were taking shape. The estate agents decided to launch the first phase. This consisted of ten houses and the units and offices to the front of the site. I was at a site meeting on the Friday of the launch with my phone on silent. I could see it was constantly flashing with missed calls and text messages. I excused myself from the meeting and stepped outside to see what was happening with all the phone activity. All the calls were from the estate agents. The first phase had sold out in less than fifteen minutes. That was over €3 million euros in sales in fifteen minutes! Crikey this development game was kind of crazy. It showed that people were willing to invest in the project and wanted to purchase what was on the market. The signs were really good as we planned to work away and release the next phase in a few months. Máirtín Óg Plant business was very busy on all fronts, apart from doing all the work for Óg Developments on our own sites we were involved in other projects with other developers and builders and I was finding it very challenging to keep up with my workload every day. My brain and my body were on overdrive. Every single decision in every aspect of what I was involved in was pulling me in every direction. While I was enjoying the constant buzz of it, I was really struggling to keep up. Physically calling to the various sites, checking in with employees and site managers and engineers, getting work signed off and agreed for payments. Organising machinery and trucks for all the various sites, drilling and blasting operations in the quarries. Finding tips or locations to dispose of excavated material. Pricing new work and dealing with general enquiries. Handling all the decisions on my own, development sites at site meetings, progress reports and targets and adherence to tight schedules and programmes. Separate meetings to attend with planners and architects and engineers, accountants and solicitors. Add to that list - meetings with AIB regarding progress and meetings with clients interested in purchasing a property or renting a unit. It was a crazy workload and a massive ship to steer with only one captain. I managed to sell one unit in the commercial building on the housing site and I had agreed a lease on two other units. The HSE were interested in the medical centre and I was in talks with a few doctors about the project also. The local Credit Union had agreed to purchase another unit in the same building. The estate agents had a list of people waiting for the release of the second phase of house units. All this along with the very quick sales after the first phase launch had the whole development project looking in good shape. The builders had asked AIB to attend one of the forthcoming site progress meetings in their Galway offices along with myself the architects and engineers.

I will never forget that cold miserable wet Friday afternoon in October 2007 at 3.50pm. I had parked outside the offices as close as I could get to the door. It was lashing rain. As I was taking my briefcase and diary out of the jeep my phone rang. It was my manager in AIB at the time. He informed me that the bank would not be attending the scheduled meeting and it had been decided that they would continue to fund the housing site development but would not fund the medical centre site any further. Oh Lord!! I discussed the situation with him briefly and his explanation made no sense to me. The decision was made at a higher level is what I was told. The bank did not want to be extended that much in Carraroe. I argued I had most of the properties either sold or rented. This banking decision had devastating consequences for the project in its entirety and for every business I was in involved in and for some of the business owners I was dealing with along with my employees. I will never understand it! What was I going to do now? I had a boardroom full of directors from the builders and my own architects and engineers waiting for me on the top floor. I felt sick and weak and powerless and useless and depleted all at the same time! This was a disaster of epic proportions. I made my way up to the boardroom and addressed the stunned audience of seven. All hell broke loose! Work was immediately stopped on both sites. Everything was fenced off and closed in. The whole project was at a standstill. The negative knock-on effect from the bank's decision was massive. The viable development I had put together and almost completely sold was now scuttled. Every business involved in the project in any way pointed the finger at me. It was my project of course. All the traffic lights at this major junction were stuck on red. It took months to get all the parties talking to see if we could structure some sort of a resolution. Meanwhile the clients who had purchased properties couldn't get them and those who were interested in purchasing or renting disappeared with all the negative vibes around the development now. The global financial downturn or crash had also begun to hit our shores. The plant company was also in deep shit. Máirtín Óg Plant and Machinery had completed a mountain of work for Óg Developments at this juncture and was therefore owed a substantial amount of money, in excess of a quarter of a million. On the back of the AIB decision not to finance the medical centre project I needed all the available funds to pay off the other creditors. The plant and machinery business had been working for other builders and developers who were also in trouble and could not afford to pay me at the time. AIB suggested I needed to come up with some cash for the shortfall to finish off the developments as I could not raise finance in any other way at this juncture, I had both businesses in the one bank of course. Remember my mother's advice! I started selling off trucks and plant that were unencumbered and pouring the money into Óg Developments. It was like pissing in the sea. I felt as if I had no choice and I really wanted to save the development project and get it across the line and deliver properties to those who had invested in the project and also do my best to get all the contractors paid to some degree. Máirtín Óg Plant and Machinery was a stable business with good equity that I had operated for over thirty years. It was now in a precarious position from selling off some of its assets along with a growing list of bad debts from creditors unable to settle their accounts, Óg Developments being one of the main ones. I had reduced the size of my plant business considerably after doing this and I was left with machinery that was on finance. Work had also dried up and rates for any available jobs were being priced at rock bottom, with the added worry of not knowing whether you would get paid or not. Having tried to soldier on for a year and a half, I made the painful decision to get out of the plant and machinery game, I pulled the plug.

By agreement with Allied Irish Leasing the last bits of plant, three diggers and two trucks were returned to their collection yard in Ashbourne, Co. Meath. This decision caused me a lot of grief. My core business for most of my life was gone, ended. I was a mess. My personal life was upside down. After twenty-five years of marriage we had separated and were now living apart. I felt under enormous pressure. It was unrelenting. Everyone looking for their pound of flesh. I had moved to Inverin, Co. Galway into a converted shed my sister Fionnuala and her husband Máirtín had provided for me. Living in a small, confined space was really difficult in the beginning. It was now my home and someplace where I could hide away from the world. I spent just over four and a half years here, it had a few other major benefits which came to light with the passing of time. My sister, Fionnuala without being too obvious about it looked out for me. She's a nurse and has a very caring nature. They lived close to the sea and I used to walk along the shoreline at all hours of the day and night. The major benefit of living next door to my sister's family home came from an unlikely source though, in the form of the three children. Ailbhe, Eoin and Niamh. They grounded me. They were in and out to me all the time. They brought me joy and laughter. I hated myself and could not even look at myself in the mirror. They loved me. The three of them rarely called in together which was better. I could focus and listen to them individually when they sat down and chatted about stuff going on in their own lives. I took great joy from listening to them and I helped them deal with their own personal issues. At a time when I felt so lost, vulnerable, desolate, lonely and unable to cope, Ailbhe, Eoin and Niamh brought a bit of magic to me and I am forever grateful for their love, kindness, friendship, laughter and affection. It meant so much to me at that time to feel loved and appreciated by these children. If you have never experienced a total devastation like this, then you may find it hard to comprehend. The pain and stress I experienced was colossal. I was sleeping very little, my mind was in constant turmoil. Every single facet of my life was falling apart. My health was suffering. I got shingles three times in the space of eighteen months, the result of dealing with chronic stress. I used to walk down to the sea at 3, 4 and 5 am and just stand there on a high rock face over the ocean in the pitch-black darkness of the night. Contemplating my situation and circumstances. Some nights it was freezing cold or pouring rain or calm with only the powerful sound of the Atlantic Ocean waves crashing against the rocks below me. I cried floods and floods of tears. I was aching inside. I could feel my whole body screaming for mercy, my mind, my heart and my stomach. I wanted the torture to end. It felt like being held in a vice and it was getting tighter by the minute. At times it was hurting to breathe. I felt so alone and deserted by everyone. All I had to do was let myself fall in as I leaned forward again and it would all end. I couldn't do it.

The strong flame I had burning within me all of my life up until now was still flickering, like a candle in the wind. I had two children and grandchildren, I needed to be here, I needed to think about others. My mother who had come through very hard times in her own life. I had three children up the road in my sister's home who loved me. I was a proud man, a person of honour someone who lived by my word and was accountable for my actions, someone who made things happen and who always helped others. I would find a way to come to terms with this excruciating existence I was living through. My phone rang one Sunday night at 9.30pm I was sitting in the dark. At this stage I was receiving fifty calls a day from creditors, debtors, solicitors, builders, contractors and so on. I always tried to answer calls or return missed calls. I never changed my number and still have the same mobile number to this day. This evening's call was my sister Angela. She listened as I informed her about my tale of woes. She then asked, "Are you drinking?" I had not touched alcohol in months. I knew it wouldn't help matters and I couldn't afford it anyway. I continued to talk for another ten minutes. Angela said "Well you haven't killed anyone". She suggested I go and talk to someone, I argued and said I would not go to a Therapist or a

Shrink or a Counsellor or any of that shit. She said I should go to a Life Coach and if I didn't agree she would call and bring me herself. I eventually agreed to go. Thanks Angela, it was the best move I could have made and probably never would have only for your call. I saw a Life Coach on many occasions, sometimes twice a week for the next few months. I slowly began to shift, small changes bit by bit. I went deep within, I started to get rid of the hurt, the past the stuff I didn't need that was serving no purpose. I began to focus on small changes and on only dealing with what I had control over. One thing at a time. I had stopped exercising completely for a year or more. I visited my GP – Dr. Michael Casey, he looked up as I entered the surgery and said "What the hell has happened to you?" I asked for something to help me cope. Michael knew me for many years and refused to put me on any medication. "Get out walking at first," he said and "gradually get back on your bike." I did and as a result of this decision and being coached at the time, the clouds began to slowly lift a bit. I thought I had one hundred friends or more but it turned out I had three. I was extremely lucky to have these guys at this very difficult and critical time for me. It wasn't so much what they said, but they took the time to call me and keep in touch and meet up for a coffee or a bit of lunch. This was invaluable for me and helped my self-esteem which was at an all-time low. If someone you know is struggling or in some sort of trouble, take the time and reach out to them. Believe me it can mean the world to that person.

In early 2006 I chanced to meet Pearse Gilroy, a Cavan man originally, now living in Dublin and working in Galway a couple of days a week. Pearse had played County Football for Cavan and we both had a keen interest in sport. He was an accountant and had a positive demeanour and attitude towards sorting stuff out. Our paths had crossed on a number of occasions. I approached him later in 2007 and we discussed my circumstances in great detail. Pearse agreed to get involved and immediately started to negotiate with all parties associated with the Carraroe development, with a view to getting the project back open and finished. I admired and really needed his professionalism, enthusiasm and positivity at this juncture. I felt like I couldn't blow out a candle. He got all sides together at different times and renegotiated terms with them all. It took many months and very skilful negotiations from Pearse to do this.

Thankfully, I still had a couple of sales pending and we used some of these pending funds to entice the builders back on site to start finishing the project. Plenty of new agreements were drawn up. I was tied up in more complicated personal guarantees and legal agreements than the massively intertwined road structure at Birmingham's Spaghetti Junction. The aerial image of its confusing myriad of intersections and slip roads, motorways and expressways was nothing compared to my shit. I had to get sealed discharges from AIB for some land and property that they were not now funding, which was almost impossible as they had funded the land purchase in the first place. The builders got first legal charge and took ownership of the medical centre building in lieu of monies owed and they were also guaranteed the proceeds of agreed sales for two units in the building. The whole process took ages and many days, weeks and hours of negotiations. Every single meeting brought up different problems and complexities. It was like riding in the grand national with difficult fences popping up all the time one after another. Eventually the project was finished but with all the uncertainty during the previous eighteen months I had lost a couple of clients and it meant five commercial units and six houses remained unsold. Why did I decide to stay involved? Why did I not run away? You might well ask. Why did I not head to another country? Disappear, grow a big beard and re-invent myself in some other place. No one would have cared. The country was in a mess in the midst of a global financial crash. What difference would it make? I was fecked anyway. Leave it to someone else to sort out, the whole thing was a mess - Spaghetti Junction! These thoughts loomed large at times, especially when I found the pressure unbearable and when other darker thoughts presented themselves to me. When I could not sleep with the feelings of helplessness, embarrassment, anxiety and shame. I had umpteen opportunities before the shit hit the fan to take money and disappear to far off places or invest in foreign property. But I never did. I was not brought up that way. I was a proud man. Believe me though, any other road except the one I chose (face the music) would have been so much easier. There was absolutely no financial gain or any benefit whatsoever for me to stay involved and sort out this situation. But I decided it was the correct and decent thing to do. My health suffered gravely at the time and caused me to require heart stents in recent years, totally as a result of the chronic stress I was dealing with during those years.

For the purposes of this book, I have gone back to revisit this period in my life. It is hugely emotional recalling these particular times and incidents. I feel the pressure in the pit of my stomach as if it was today. I have shed many tears again today as I type. I have walked away out of the house on four different occasions since 6.30am. It feels like I am tearing old wounds apart and it feels uncomfortable and painful and very raw twelve/thirteen years later. To imagine myself being in that state, feeling so low and in such a dark place on many occasions is frightening. I took it so personally and so final for such a long time and I kept dragging myself down continuously. I made mistakes and wrong decisions for sure when under extreme pressure. Stress of any kind is lethal, chronic stress in personal and business matters can be fatal. Luckily my mental health did not suffer even though my whole body and mind were under severe pressure. I have always had great mental strength when I needed to call on it or dip into it if you like. I managed to dig deep within myself to find and tap into my inner core strength. I have gone to that well many times now in my life, in personal, business, sporting and extreme challenges. That flame that burns deep within me. Some people never find it. I firmly believe that we all have it. Others never need to go to that place and manage to slide through life without ever having to go that deep. Do these people live boring uneventful lives? Circumstances and the cards you are dealt to play can have a huge influence on your life. Death or serious illness, losing a job, separation, divorce or the end of a long relationship, physical or mental abuse, addiction, trying to lose weight, any type of change or a pandemic. The list goes on and on.

Many people in high profile stressful jobs are dealing with the same. Single adults and young teens. If you are suffering in any way or feel under pressure, the best advice I can give you is to reach out to someone, a friend or a professional person in whatever area you feel you need help. Do not wait for tomorrow or next week or next month. I reached out and it kick started my recovery and helped me get through my difficulties. Self-care is crucial in today's environment more than ever. We cannot fix ourselves without help and it is perfectly ok and cool to ask for help. It is also extremely important and critical to talk to another human being that you trust. Whether it is to help you in your career, business or private life. Don't be existing. – start living.

Mam & Dad after the 1966 All Ireland – Galway Won

Galway Under 21 team – 1981 All Ireland Finalists

NCBI – USA Coast to Coast Team 2000

Excavation for the Eyre Square Centre Development 1990

Grandad Willy & my Dad and Uncle Tom

Dad in his Morris Minor (James Dean Style)

Dad in his Commer Truck

Mam and me at the beach

Myself, Eoin, Ailbhe and Niamh (my sister Fionnula's children)

Deep Excavation at Rossaveal

**Me and Sean Kelly on the famous Alp
d'Huez climb, France**

Me and my son Sean on Mount Everest 2018

**Me and my son Sean on Mount Everest
having reached Base Camp 2018**

Me and my partner Delores in Scotland   Me in a pensive mood

My mother Tess, my son Sean and myself in Connemara

Making the cover of the NCBI magazine with John Mannion

On top of Carrauntoohil with our hiking group 2019

81

My Uncles Peter and Colm, my Mom and Dad, my Aunts, Eena and Nuala

Mother and whole Family (All 7 together)
Top row, left to right: Máirtín Óg, Ciarán, Gabriel
Bottom Row, left to right; Ursula, Angela, Tess, Fionnula and Tish and Roxie the
dog (missing from photo Bailey the other dog)

Chapter 6

I NEVER LOST MY DIGNITY

"Never take a person's dignity. It's worth everything to them and nothing to you". – Frank Barron Prof. of Psychology.

"Humility is the ability to give up your pride and still retain your dignity".
— Vanna Bonta, Italian-American writer.

"To lose face." The phrase originated in China. A person who loses face feels that his status is diminished and that he has lost the respect of others. That was me!! Jayzuz lads I was in a bad place, I was doomed, wiped out.... My family were doubting me, in some cases blaming me, friends fell away and disappeared as if I had the plague, business associates were running for cover, banks were pushing and pushing, creditors wanted payments, clients wanted answers. Debtors could not afford to pay me. I was my own biggest debtor with my development company. In other words, my long established plant and machinery company – Máirtín Óg Plant was owed more money by Óg Developments than any other business I was dealing with. I was buckling under the enormous pressure. I couldn't sleep. Receiving heaps of phone calls and questions, inquisition after inquisition. I was the general of a falling army, the captain of the titanic, the leader of a doomed expedition, the last man standing. Every part of my life was smashed to smithereens - into tiny pieces and scattered around me. Everything was completely broken. I was broken. My businesses were gone, my employees and my marriage, my circle of friends and associates and my family. My income and any hope of turning things around. It was too late for that. I could not look at myself in the mirror. Whatever could go wrong did go wrong. Problems and heartaches in life are inevitable. I was trying all the usual things. Telling myself I can control this, I have dealt with worse, this too shall pass, some things are improving, some are out of my control. I went to a few different churches and visited many graveyards in search of solutions and looking for answers and advice on what to do next.

I did not want to admit it but my health was beginning to suffer as well. The battle to get out of rock bottom would take time and every ounce of energy I had. I struggle now today as I type out this chapter and remember those feelings and the enormity and scale of what I was facing. I was at the edge of my life, at the door of surrender and staring death in the face. That is how I was feeling, in the tight grip of despair and desolation. Today I feel uncomfortable at those thoughts and feelings from that time in my life, created by writing this book. Recently I spoke to a friend who buried his young teen son after illness and eventually a sudden death. Over the course of a few hours we discussed pain, sorrow and emptiness and the blank space in your heart. He didn't cry but I did. It reminded me of "that pain" I had experienced and still do from time to time. The trauma I have had to deal with and the outfall I still mask over every day. We talked about the reminders, birthdays, special occasions, the trigger points that get you going, the memories, or a sad song or a photograph or simply a thought. I tried to console him in the only way I knew, explaining how I dealt with my pain. It gets easier with time I said. I lied, it never gets easier, you get better at dealing with it, you console yourself by eventually realising and admitting it was not your fault and you stop blaming yourself. That does bring a degree of comfort that allows you to move on. For many years I have had nagging feelings of insecurity, fear, sadness, shame, responsibility and failure. Overwhelming feelings of letting people down and even acceptance of blame. When you've lost everything and you are attempting to start your life over again these negative emotions can gain the upper hand.

This can make you feel trapped and you end up self – sabotaging, having anxiety and feeling overwhelmed. Processing thoughts like, a few short months ago I was worth a whole pile of millions, I had opportunities and possibilities, I was steering projects and big construction jobs, a work force, a scatter of plant and machinery, development lands and planning applications. I also had a good income, security and stability and a family life and a home. Then everything changed drastically.

We need to slow down here and take stock. One part of this story is about a man losing his businesses and his livelihood, properties and assets. The other part concerns a man who has lost his identity and his confidence, his family and friends. I will ask you to pause here and try to imagine yourself in this position in this situation. Who you are at this moment and what you do? Your career, business, relationship, family, friends, associates, your home and income are all gone. How would you cope? How would you survive? What would you do next or where would you find some answers? I hear you say - it would never happen, I wouldn't let it get to that stage.

One never knows what road lies ahead. An accident or illness, a financial crisis, a pandemic or something unexpected, or some other drastic change to your circumstances and before you know it you're struggling to cope and adapt just like myself. Attempting to cope with loss of any kind brings us into contact with grief. It's very important to acknowledge this and then find a way to manage it. People who experience and suffer the death of a loved one may have to deal with the same feelings and emotions. Those who suffer an injury, severe or otherwise, we feel it when someone gets a dire diagnosis or the thought of losing a parent. Coping with a virus or pandemic can bring on the same feelings. Things become uncertain and we don't feel safe. What was normal no longer is, our thoughts go into overdrive, we're not sure what to do or what the future is and we don't feel safe. Anxiety begins to take a grip. Emotions can run riot, denial or sadness is how we cope but, in my experience, neither work. Acceptance is where the strength can be found. That doesn't make it any easier and it can be very difficult especially in the beginning and can be very painful if you attempt to force it. Try to prioritise what's important now – at this moment in time. I do this regularly if and when I find myself faced with the possibility of loss or a difficult challenge or situation. Ground yourself, whatever works for you to do this. Meditate, head into nature, go for a walk, phone a friend, stamp your feet, sing a song, look around you and appreciate what is in your surroundings and the people in your life that matter to you. Bring yourself into the present moment and situation. Find a balance between those thoughts in your head, or those two balancing on your shoulder, in my case Mr. Doubt and Mr. Suffer) between what has happened and what could happen.

Negative thoughts are like weeds that strangle confidence. You're in control of your own thoughts and your own actions. You hold your own reins. Mr. Doubt and Mr. Suffer have been with me on my shoulders for almost forty years now. I discovered and named them in my early twenties. We have soldiered together in all my many battles and adventures and in every success. They bring a mix of good and bad which adds to the balance I think. Mr. Doubt presents himself just to check in and see if I'm committed and certain of my plans and decisions. The other lad always appears so he can test me, it's like he's checking to see if I am worthy of success or capable of completing the challenge, or ready to give up. We have a cordial relationship nowadays and I actually expect and welcome their input and I have given them pride of place resting on my shoulders. They force me to dig deep, they cause me to question my commitment, my drive and my passion. They flag the dangers and the pain and suffering associated with life and decision making. They are good guys but very lazy, they don't like challenges or decision making or training and preparation. I totally acknowledge their existence and listen to what they have to say. Then I go to my intuition, to that place in my stomach, to my gut to find my answers and that is the compass that directs me.

"We may encounter many defeats, but we must not be defeated" – Maya Angelou, poet and writer.

I was not going to run away, a consideration but not an option for me. My intention was to deal with this somehow and come out the other side. You may not have had the experience of having lost everything as I did, but you may feel stuck or you may have lost someone in your life, or you may be dealing with difficult circumstances of some kind and you can identify with what I am saying. When you experience loss or failure or the breakdown of something you have worked hard at for a long period of time it can be very difficult to accept and come to terms with. Your negative thoughts and emotions kick into gear and can become your reality. You start to blame yourself and depending on the scale of what has transpired for you, it can feel like you're stuck in quicksand and can't get out. The sense of hopelessness starts to take hold. Whether you're dealing with financial problems, family conflict, or work-related issues, struggles in life are inevitable. Overcoming these things is never easy. Blame is a monster especially if you accept it. Some people become victims and blame others or circumstances or conditions. I do not claim to be an expert in this field in any way.

I am speaking from my own life experience and what I have seen since becoming a Life Coach.

I have read countless articles and researched 'self-blame'. My experience of it is centred in particular around the time I had my difficulties from 2007 onwards and up to as recent as June 2021. Self-blame is known to be a common reaction to stressful events. I found that multiple factors in my environment were putting demands on me that I was unable to cope with. I could not change the events or the conditions, and not being able to do so caused conflict within me. I could not plan or achieve anything, even short-term goals were unattainable. As a sports man and an adventure enthusiast I have been in many stressful situations and circumstances. I perform very well in these scenarios, but this is a different environment. Climbing big mountains in bad weather conditions when you have to assess the dangers and the safety measures while trying to achieve your goal and lead a group. Facing a gruelling endurance event and dealing with changing conditions and the mental challenges going on inside your head. Planning a big construction job or leading a team, all of this stuff is second nature to me. In 2007 and for the next few years many things were out of my control. I could not change or influence the outcome in any way, and I could not change the circumstances. I did not plan this crash or the resultant outfall. It was time to refocus and gather the pieces of my life strewn all over the place. I had to pick out what was required and relevant and I needed to discard the rest. Realising that I must take some positive action and improve my mental and physical health was the start of the process, actually doing so was an entirely different matter.

Mindset, willpower and persistence have always been some of my strongest traits. I have a growth mindset.

Some of the benefits of which are being open minded, comfortable with ambiguity and uncertainty, show strong situational awareness and take ownership. Persistence is having power of will and power of desire. With the benefit of Life Coaching and harnessing my natural strengths I started to put some structures in place. I went back to basics and took a constructive look at my circumstances. I began to accept what had occurred and I also focused on dealing with whatever issues I could one at a time. Prior to this the enormity of the situation was dragging me down. It sounds so logical and the only sensible way to deal with things, but when you get caught up in your own shit it can seem overwhelming. You freeze and feel unable to make any decision because of a mixture of fear and apprehension and uncertainty. Finding a logical clear pathway for moving forward appears impossible. I started to mark out this pathway and by slowly achieving small wins every day, my outlook and energy started to improve. I began exercising again, taking daily walks by the sea which helped me hugely.

I cannot over emphasise the importance of this. Getting out in the fresh air and walking along the seashore was repairing me, some days I cried, I was sad and felt weary and the weight of what I was carrying was like a backpack full of bricks. Each one of us is carrying our own backpack. As a Life Coach I ask clients to remove some of those bricks that are not required anymore and make room for some new lighter bricks. These heavy bricks can be specific, judgments, limiting beliefs, painful memories, unchecked thoughts, harmful habits or denied emotions. It's important to remember that these bricks are not real. They are just perception, just thoughts. They come and go. At times they feel really heavy and other times they just float away out of your mind. I threw my own bricks on the ground and went through them many mornings while on my walks and I flung the ones I no longer needed into the sea. On numerous occasions I did this and I always came back feeling lighter and with a bit more energy and enthusiasm. The combination of the small wins and the exercise was having a hugely positive effect on me. My sleeping pattern began to improve. I was managing a few hours of uninterrupted sleep most nights. Three friends who had stayed in contact were meeting up with me for coffee and chats regularly and this also helped my confidence. The raging storm had calmed down considerably and was showing signs of disappearing. I managed to hold on to my dignity during this time.

I behaved in a dignified manner at all times showing great self-respect and respect for others. I was let down by many and treated unfairly, while it hurt at the time, I put it down to people's misunderstanding, being ill informed and jumping to conclusions.

The old Irish saying – "An té atá thuas óltar deoch air."
An té atá thíos buailtear cós air."The one who is successful is toasted. The one who is down is kicked".

Business related meetings and any dealings associated with the two companies was not easy during this time. I always took calls and attended meetings and tried to deal with issues to the best of my ability. I never closed the door on any enquiry or problem. I was as honest and honourable as I could be under the circumstances. When you are confronted with difficult situations and circumstances, whether it's in relationships or your career or business it can be a struggle to remain dignified. We start to see ourselves as tainted, unworthy or inadequate from the lack of dignity and respect we feel from others. Our self-image and self-perception can become skewed. We condemn and judge ourselves harshly. We don't give ourselves self-love or self-nurturing, self-care or self-respect. We stop prioritising our wellbeing. Our outlook on life, our self-perception and the rest of the world can also become tainted. We feel like we have no support and our environment is a cruel place. We feel more pessimistic about the chances of recovery and getting out of the hole we are in. Our negative thought patterns absolutely start to take over and we become increasingly negative and cynical about the world around us. When we are robbed of our dignity, we feel insecure and even self- hating and afraid of interactions with people that might make us feel bad about ourselves, so we retreat inward and away from places where we might feel threatened. As I recall these feelings I realise how frail my self- perception and mental health was at that particular juncture. I was condemning and judging myself all the time in a form of self-abandonment. I felt black and blue from literally beating myself up. It's very important to realise that thoughts are not facts, remembering this can help lessen the power of these negative thinking patterns.

I had to be strong and counter these feelings and forces and cultivate my dignity and self-respect. I needed to love and accept myself. Very often we try to escape this pain by using drugs or booze and other unhealthy coping mechanisms. We self-medicate and our addictions and mental health issues flourish in these circumstances. Luckily for me I did not go down this road. I went to the outdoors and towards exercise and took on a Life Coach. I began to rebuild my own self-esteem, my sense of self-worth, my sense of pride in myself. I started to respect and honour myself as a human being. I believed I was worthy of respect, I was proud of my abilities, my qualities and my achievements. I believed I could rebuild, I accepted my mistakes. I stopped worrying about the opinions of others and stayed true to my own core beliefs and values. I started to change my -self perceptions and that of others. I held myself accountable to continue to live like this. My circumstances had indeed changed enormously but I was still me. I went back to my beliefs, my core values and started making goals for myself, small targets to aim for every day. Adversity can come in many forms in your life. So how do you react? Are you angry and disappointed, ranting and raving to yourself and anyone who will listen? Feeling dejected and victimised and resigned to the situation? You go through multiple emotional states as you try to deal with the mess. I believe it's then you need to step up and turn your initial reaction around and counter adversity with resilience. This dynamic is central to my life and all the challenges I have overcome.

Psychological resilience is the capacity to respond quickly and constructively to crises. It's at the core of most survival stories. It can be hard to muster for different reasons, fear, anger, and confusion can paralyse us after a severe setback. Humans tend to assign blame rather than generating solutions. Attempting to summit a mountain takes a lot of planning and preparation, the correct gear and favourable weather. On many occasions you may have to decide to turn back due to inclement weather, dangerous terrain, bad health or illness or some unexpected event or circumstances. After all the effort of getting to this place you have to abort the expedition and go back down to safety and plan to return another time. I have made this decision many times as a resilient individual, it's about moving from analysis to a plan of action and reaction. When adversity strikes at our door, we usually fall into one of two emotional traps. Deflation is one I certainly felt and had to deal with. I was used to success and able to fix problems and make things happen. The trauma I was going through and dealing with brought me back to reality with a bang, setting off intense bursts of negative emotion, like a dark cloud had settled around me. The other one is victimisation, In the face of an adverse event(s) many of us assume the role of helpless bystander. We start to blame everyone and everything as the cause of our difficulties. When we can dip into our resilience, we have the ability to recover from or adjust easily to misfortune or change, or the ability to become strong, healthy or successful again after something bad happens. In sport, the requirement to bounce back from adversity is key to long-term success. To some, resilience is like a miracle drug, a personality trait that can heal all wounds and right all wrongs. It is a wonderful trait to possess and relates to a lot of positive outcomes. The definition of resilience from Psychology Today is described in this way: "Resilience is that ineffable quality that allows some people to be knocked down by life and come back stronger than ever. Rather than letting failure overcome them and drain their resolve, they find a way to rise from the ashes" – the ability to bounce back. Resilience is commonly associated with "mental toughness" – a personality trait that determines how individuals deal with stress, pressure and challenge irrespective of circumstances. It's part hardiness and part confidence.

Grit also comes into the equation. Grit is the tendency to stick with something long-term, no matter how difficult it is or how many roadblocks you face. Another one is mental endurance, the inner strength we use to deal with our challenges. It requires willpower, self-discipline and perseverance to develop and maintain. The last one is fortitude, the strength of mind that enables a person to encounter danger or bear pain or adversity with courage. Resilience and all its traits is not only for the most inspiring, impressive and awesome among us, it's surprisingly common. Research has shown that resilience is ordinary not extraordinary. It's about experiencing all of the negative, difficult and distressing events that life throws at you and staying on task, optimistic and high functioning. We all have it and some of us are more resilient than others. We have all been knocked down, defeated and despondent at some stage in our lives. How you deal with these things and especially how you untangle your thoughts and beliefs about it and shifting how you respond determines your bounce back ability. For most of us after we experience a difficult episode of some sorts, we make quick assumptions about the causes, magnitude, consequences and duration. Building resilience does not happen when things are going well and you have no problems. It's best done precisely when times are tough and things are difficult, when we face many challenges and we are at the greatest risk of misfiring with our reaction, and when we cannot see the opportunities being presented. Many miss this opportunity for growth. Their mindset does not allow them to control unproductive responses to adversity. They revert to victimisation or deflation and miss the chance to replace negativity with creativity and resourcefulness. Resilience is a long-term fitness plan, not a crash diet. It's the difference between facing your problems bravely and confidently and feeling helpless and like you can't move on. Being involved in sport I believe is a big advantage in this area of resilience. At an early age you learn how to be a team player and the ethos of trying to be part of a successful team. In team sport and individual events, you learn how to prepare and train and apply yourself, you learn the rules and regulations and how to adapt to different conditions and pressures. Most importantly you learn how to react and cope with loss and disappointment. You appreciate that you will not win every time and that you can go away take stock improve and come back again and again. You also understand that you experience days when it all goes very well and that other days can be disastrous. You develop an appreciation and respect for being able to take part. You learn how to deal with disappointments and injuries and how to rehab and return to participate again. You also work on your- self-development, motivation and commitment.

You become more resilient with each experience. I recently heard an interview by Ronan O'Gara, the retired Munster and Irish Rugby player and current head coach and director of rugby at La Rochelle. In the interview clip he talks about pressure and dealing with the responsibility of being the goal kicker on the team very often faced with the prospect of kicking the winning points or missing and losing the match. He mentions the Heineken Cup Final in 2000 - Munster V Northampton. O'Gara did not score that day having had five attempts, the "demons hit him" as he put it. "Real pressure hits you twice a season, it'll get you. But it's a real opportunity to grow and get better". The score in that final saw Northampton win the game 9 – 8. It took him a long, long time to get over it. He wasn't able for it for a long time. But in due course and with the benefit of experience he grew to love that pressure and responsibility. In my own case I remember playing for Galway in the Minor (under18) Connacht Football Final V Mayo in 1978, I did not play well, the occasion got to me. Mayo won that match and went on to become All Ireland Champions. In 1981 - I played in the All Ireland under 21 Final V Cork, it finished in a draw and Cork went on to beat us in the replay. Again, it was not my finest hour. I was taken off and reintroduced again in the second half in the drawn game. I had performed very well in all other matches during both campaigns and qualifying for those respective finals. In his book Legacy, author James Kerr immersed himself with the All Blacks rugby team for a couple of months. In Chapter 1X: Pressure.- he discusses pressure from an All Black perspective – "pressure is expectation, scrutiny and consequence". Under pressure your attention is either diverted or on track. If diverted, you have a negative emotional response which leads to unhelpful behaviour. That means you're stuck, that means you're overwhelmed. On the other hand, if your attention is on track, you have situational awareness and you execute accurately. You are clear, you adapt and you overcome.

The same applies in business and everyday life. Like O'Gara I have grown and learnt from these and other experiences, and over the years I have improved at managing my thoughts and attention. You respond instead of reacting. Where we direct our minds, is where our thoughts will take us, those thoughts create emotions, which define our behaviour, which defines our performance. By controlling our attention and our thoughts we can manage our emotions and enhance our performance. When running any business, you face up to challenges and pressures on a regular basis. Some leaders are good at dealing with these issues in certain areas but not on all fronts. It's important to realise this and seek help and advice and avoid being overwhelmed and stuck.

A leader must create clarity and not confusion. In your career it's also vital to handle this expectation, scrutiny and consequence. When you have situational awareness, you are clear, you adapt and overcome. Bad decisions are made by an inability to handle pressure at the critical moment. You are operating in the dark. The All Blacks refer to the dark as Red Head and the light as Blue Head. I love this analogy and I believe it's very true in life as well as sport.

Keeping a Red Head, you're in the dark, you are tight, inhibited, desperate, aggressive, anxious, results-oriented and overcompensating. You are in a negative loop of self-judgement, aggression, shut down and panic.

Keeping a Blue Head, you are in the light, you're loose, expressive, calm, clear, accurate, in the moment, on task. You are in a state of deep calmness and you are on task, in the zone, on your game, in control and in a state of flow. Staying in the blue takes practice and commitment and a very strong mindset. Pressure comes in many forms whether it's life/work/exams, you can be a sports person, a business leader or manager or a parent juggling priorities. Managing stress is relevant to all situations. Keep your focus on what you can control and the areas you can affect and change. We all tend to look at the areas we are least likely to be able to change or control when we find ourselves under pressure and overwhelmed. By determining where you focus your attention, you focus on an area where you can affect some change and gain some clarity and start taking command of the situation. Transforming from a "Red Head to a Blue Head" can help you cope better with the pressure and get you performing to the best of your ability. Maintaining a "Blue Head" in all areas of your life is the real goal. You're in a state of flow and operating with a cool head and calmness while still being very much in the zone and at your best.

"I realised my greatest strength was not my physical ability, it was my mental ability" – Bruce Jenner.

Chapter 7

I CARVED MY PLACE IN FOREIGN LANDS

I went to Nepal and Mount Everest in 2018 and found it hugely emotional and spiritual. It was a defining time for me. I made the decision to go on December 21st 2017. My partner Dolores and I, had been to the Travellers Inn (Elaine Fahy's) around the corner from the house for a few drinks and had continued at home with a night cap. Jameson for me, It helps me plan ahead! Towards the back end of 2017 I was planning my goals and adventures for the following year. I'm going to do two events in 2018 I proclaimed. I normally decide on my options every Christmas for the year ahead.

Gran Fondo New York (GFNY) which started off with just one event in New York is now a cycling race series of sixteen events taking place around the world. The New York edition or GFNY is a 100 – mile route from NYC to Bear Mountain and back. Event date May 19th, 2018. It starts on the George Washington Bridge and rides North following the Hudson River upstream on rural roads and through scenic towns. Taking in the Palisades and up Route 9W. Climbing Bear Mountain with views of the entire Hudson Valley. More challenging climbs as you make your way through picturesque Rockland County back to the Palisades and to the finish line at Fort Lee. A Gran Fondo is an Italian term which loosely translates to "Big Ride". Basically, take a scenic mountainous course and add several thousand cyclists ranging from pros and amateurs to beginners. Include mechanical and medical support, electronic timing, feed zones manned by cheerful volunteers serving up healthy snacks, fruit and drinks, and traffic halted at junctions and rolling road closures and supportive spectators lining the course and a fun post-race party. Add in energy, excitement and atmosphere - this is a Gran Fondo. My cousin Earnán Naughton had suggested we do it together along with a few friends. Dolores committed to do the shorter 50 mile route and that was her goal for May 2018. We would do some training together I suggested.

Next on my agenda – hiking to Everest Base Camp. Everest is much more than a mountain and the journey to its base camp is more than a trek. As close to the top of the world as you can get without altitude experience. I had been doing some hiking in the Burren on my doorstep, but for Everest Base Camp I would need to up my game. I was excited to be committed to these two totally different challenges for the year ahead. I can always focus and apply myself to any challenge once I have a goal and a set date to work towards. Planning and goal setting is a part of life for everyone, most of us make plans and set our goals on a daily basis. However not everyone is successful at this. I see many struggle with mundane everyday things like controlling food intake, reducing alcohol consumption, getting enough quality sleep, getting up in time and planning the day ahead well in advance, limiting TV viewing or social media. Everyday normal stuff that makes up our daily lives. Managing that is the equivalent of climbing a mountain for many. Getting on top of and at the same time in control of your decision making is a skill or an art if you like. That sounds lovely and looks great written down but is much more difficult than that. Or is it? Why do some find it so difficult to manage their lives and retain the correct balance, to figure out what is good for them and what is not. To look deep within and make decisions that feel right for themselves to choose their own desired path. Where are you on your own journey?

Mindset is the crucial element for me in my life. "Mindset matters it can feed or impede your actions".

According to Stanford psychologist Carol Dweck, your beliefs play a pivotal role in what you want and whether you achieve it. Dweck has found through her extensive research that it is your mindset that plays a significant role in determining achievement and success. Your mindset is a set of beliefs that shape how you make sense of the world and yourself. It influences how you feel, think and behave in any given situation. There are two basic mindsets according to Dweck, fixed and growth. If you are a fixed mindset type, you believe your abilities are fixed traits and therefore can't be changed. You may also believe that your talent and intelligence alone leads to success, and effort is not required. On the other hand, if you have a growth mindset, you believe that your talents and abilities can be developed over time through effort and persistence.

My experience in all aspects of my life has been that my growth mindset over time with hard work and persistence has helped me achieve and succeed. The Christmas of 2017 saw me commit to taking on two very distinct challenges for the coming year. I had completed many cycling endurance events, so 100 miles in one day on a hilly circuit in New York was nothing really new. Everest Base Camp was a totally different story. The only experience I had with hiking or trekking was going for long walks! This one excited me. I was attempting a different discipline, learning how my body was going to react to getting up mountains and descending back down. Regardless of what you set out to do in your life, you must respect it. Respect and appreciate the process, prepare to the best of your ability. Change, adapt, learn, push, stumble, fall and get up again. There is no hidden secret no magic formula.

"Great works are performed not by strength but by perseverance" – *Samuel Johnson.*

December 2017 was when I decided to go ahead with these challenges and early December 2017 was when I started my preparation. I was never really a New Year resolution kind of guy, what is that all about? Why wait for a date on the calendar? Get started and ease yourself into it has always been my mentality. So I did. When the world rolled into 2018, I already had some miles in my legs (as they say in cycling) and I had started to hike for longer durations and in hilly terrain. I had a vision and to help me attain that vision, I had focused my mindset and my goals on what needed to happen to work towards that vision. I have learned though, that moderation is also a hugely valuable and key quality. The Cambridge Dictionary describes moderation as the quality of doing something within reasonable limits.

Overdoing anything leads to tiredness, frustration, anxiety, anger, breakdown and stress. To do, to use, or stress to excess, carry something too far, to do something to an excessive degree, we often fall into this in our daily lives. It is a very fine line, a delicate balance between what is required or enough and what's actually overdoing it. I have managed to find my balance and what works for me. When preparing for any event this is of huge significance. Whether it's your personal life, business, career or from a sporting context. Training for Gran Fondo New York (GFNY) and Everest Base Camp (EBC) I needed to be very aware of overtraining, of over stretching myself, of keeping my work, my relationships, my health and wellbeing in perfect balance. This delicate balance in life is considerably difficult to attain. If you over commit to a particular area in your life, other parts will begin to suffer the consequences. If you are heavily committed to your work, business or career, it will take a toll on your relationships, your family and your own health and wellbeing. In sport or business those who are over committed generally try to do much more than is humanly possible, and they use up all their energy in the process, to the point that they get sick, exhausted and in poor health. I have seen and dealt with the consequences of pushing the limits from both a work and sporting perspective. Fatigue, lack of energy, underperforming, injury and no motivation. Dealing with this form of stress has a big effect on your mental and physical health over time. I compare it to keeping the balance on a seesaw. Not too much either side. The magic of finding a personal dimmer switch, so you are not fully on or fully off.

"Life's challenges aren't here to break you. Life's challenges are here to mold, refine and make you into all you were intended to become".
– Billy Cox, author and motivational speaker.

When training in the mountains I quickly realised that my descending off the steeper slopes was crap. I was slow and my footing was unsure and I didn't have any confidence especially on technical descents. I had a dodgy knee and my core strength was nowhere near where it needed to be. My knee injury may have ended my county football career prematurely, but I never let it stop me doing anything else in life. With the cycling I had built up the muscles around my knee joint which gave me some stability, however I always needed to manage it and be aware of how far I could push without causing more damage. I can cycle for hundreds of miles in a day or for weeks without any knee issues, however I can go to a party or a wedding, do a lot of dancing (which I have been known to do) and end up walking with a limp or painful knee joint the following day. Too much sideways movement does not suit my damaged knee joint. Coming down off the high mountains especially the technical descents was causing problems. I started a gym programme with Robbie Lane at Doc Fitness and the results were instant. My core began to get stronger and I was soon descending with confidence. As the weeks rolled into months I was really getting into great shape. I was spending long hours in the saddle, three early mornings a week in the gym and also doing some long hard hikes. I was combining long 100/200 kms rides with short faster efforts occasionally. I was mixing up the hiking with five/ten hour efforts in the hills and long six/eight hours on the flat carrying heavy weights in my backpack. The gym three days a week was improving my physique and core gradually. When your performance starts to improve and you begin to see positive changes and progress being made, it's like a drug. You begin to feel real positive energy from yourself and what you are doing. It's the same in everyday life, if you set goals and start to make changes for yourself. You start to improve and adjust the balance between your work or career and the rest of your life. Your family life, your relationships, your health and wellbeing all start to show signs of improvement. Once the changes start to kick in you will start to experience the same feelings. It's a mindset change and the results are phenomenal. The only thing you need to be careful of and very aware of is moderation. As I mentioned, holding and maintaining that very delicate balance between over doing it and nailing it. I am a lifelong student of this art and have learned to recognise the trigger signs and therefore adjust accordingly. Loss of motivation, or low energy levels, feeling tired and fatigued, getting irritated and narky are all signs that you need to pull back a bit and give your body a chance to recover mentally as well as physically. Listen to your body, pay attention to what it is saying to you and treat it accordingly.

My son Seán had popped down to Kinvara for a visit in the spring. While shooting the breeze over a few whiskies our discussion veered towards my Everest expedition. The discussion finished late into the night with Seán agreeing to also take up the challenge. He still does not remember giving the commitment! This was brilliant as Seán and myself trained regularly together and encouraged one another (it was nicely competitive at times). As a father it was fantastic to be heading to the highest mountain on the planet with my son. In all my escapades in my life's journey to date I have rarely been in the company of anyone who I have felt 100% comfortable with and able to trust completely. Seán is one of those rare individuals. In this type of environment he possesses huge physical and mental ability. He is physically and mentally very strong and combines those attributes with a quick practical thinking brain and a great attitude. He is also full of devilment and crack.

We are a great team. I convinced Seán to join me on a visit to the 'Anatomy and Human Performance Laboratory' at Trinity College Dublin for VO2max and Lactate threshold testing. The importance of this testing I have discussed in detail in Chapter 4. It was a great barometer for both of us, as to where our fitness levels were and what we needed to concentrate on for a successful expedition to Everest. The tests showed that I was in great shape and my stats were impressive according to Bernard Donne, the same man that had tested me eighteen years earlier before the USA Coast to Coast cycle. He complimented me on how I was maintaining my fitness and keeping myself in great order and especially for coming back again to be tested. Seán was told that while his results were good, he still needed to up his endurance capacity. He accepted this advice from Bernard and I paid the price for the next few months. Seán was working and living in Dublin and began to cycle to and from work and go for long walks carrying a backpack loaded up with weights. When we trained together he was now putting me under huge pressure!!

I headed to Majorca from April 4th to the 11th 2018 for a solid week of cycling to get some long spins done day after day. I have been going to the island for many years and worked as a guide for SUNVELO, a cycling holiday company based in Playa de Muro on the North Coast near the Port of Alcudia. Majorca has become a favourite destination for an estimated 150,000 cyclists from all over the world every year. The industry is worth around €150 million according to a recent European Union-funded study. There are plenty of very good bike shops, coffee shops, bars and the best of hotels offering great services and welcoming the cycling community with open arms. Smooth winding mountain roads, testing climbs, coastal routes, quiet winding valley roads through vineyards and very cycling friendly locals and an accommodating climate all mean that Majorca is the perfect location for cycling holidays and training camps for amateurs and professional cycling teams who base themselves here early in the season. Despite its popularity, many of the roads are still pleasantly quiet, local government quickly realised the island had potential to become a cycling paradise and invested in infrastructure and road surfacing. The monstrous Majorca 312 cyclo-sportive attracts thousands of riders each year. It's a 312 kilometre lap of the entire island and not for the faint hearted, taking in over 5,000 metres of climbing as you move along the circumference of the island. You are given twelve hours to complete the epic cycle. I managed to finish it on three occasions, my best time being just under ten hours. After my hard week of training in Majorca I felt ready for the trip to New York to ride Gran Fondo NY (GFNY). All I had to do was keep myself ticking over for a few weeks.

Friday April 18th, 2018 our group of six riders landed in John F. Kennedy International Airport, New York. Arriving Friday allowed a few days to acclimatise, get the bikes ready and prepare for the event on Sunday April 20th, 2018. GFNY is a 100 mile personal endurance challenge where you compete against others, the clock and yourself. The 100 mile event is capped at 5,000 riders, there is also a 50 mile ride capped at 1,000 riders. Double

Tree, Hilton Hotel, Fort Lee, New Jersey was the chosen base for the weekend. It was close to the start compared to other hotels in New York City. Like most all day events, you needed to pick up your race pack ahead of time. This was taking place in a public building across from NY Penn Station. It took forty-five minutes to get through the long lines waiting to sign on for the event and pick up the numbers, special official jersey, water bottle, coffee mug, bottle of wine, guidebook/route notes, race bib and timing chip and a wrist band for access to the feed zones/toilets/showers etc. for the event. We rounded off the evening with a nice meal at the Double Tree and a few beers and some interesting conversation with other cyclists also staying there, some who had participated in the event before. It was nice to compare experiences from cycling events in different parts of Europe, USA and so on. I settled in for a good night's sleep to finish off the Friday. Saturday morning we awoke to heavy rain, Sunday was also forecast as misty and wet for the morning with a possibility of thunderstorms for Sunday afternoon!! For Saturday after putting the bikes together and checking that everything was in smooth working order and inflating the tyres to the desired pressures, it was time for a slow lunch and some relaxation. I tend to favour this approach before big events, getting as much rest as possible and conserving energy. Others like to sight see or walk around and visit different points of interest. My motto is - if you can sit, don't stand, if you can lie down, don't sit, if you can chill, don't panic. Conserve as much energy as possible, stay out of draughts, stay in from the rain, keep cool from the sun, stay away from or turn off the air conditioning. Keep hydrated and enjoy the relaxing atmosphere you create as part of the build-up. Stay in your zone. Sunday May 20th, 2018 at 5.05am Dolores and I stepped out of the lift with our bikes and into the lobby of the Fort Lee Hotel. The place was buzzing with cyclists busily making final adjustments, stocking up on food and water. We followed a group outside to jump in behind a scheduled 5.15am police escort to the start. When we exited the hotel doors, the escort was already leaving out of sight 5 minutes early! Time for plan B. Many more cyclists were starting to make their way to the George Washington Bridge and the official start line, we just followed all the riders in the green and black official event kit and after crossing over pedestrian/bike bridges, taking a few turns, a good descent and a ride, back up a steep incline, we got on to the GWB at 6.20am for the 7am start. It was dark and rather cold, temperature a cool 62 degrees Fahrenheit. We were all grouped into corrals of five hundred by race numbers and the atmosphere was at fever pitch. We were on the lower deck of the bridge and you could hear the traffic overhead and the vibrations coming from the upper deck. Loud music and the official announcements along with 5,000 cyclists in green and black jerseys, flashing red and amber lights, nervous tension and excitement, altogether a fabulous cauldron. At 7am on the button the massive loud hooter was sounded and the event was under way. It took a bit of time to drop the gates for all the various corrals and get every rider away. Like any mass start event GFNY was no different. As the adrenalin kicks in riders plough away from the gun with no consideration for the sheer numbers on tight roads. Within 200 yards we passed cyclists on the deck, the tarmac was extremely slippery from the rain fall and the road narrowed with some bollards on each side and a slight descent as we got down on to Henry Hudson Drive. My bike handling skills are fairly good but in these situations someone can collapse straight in front of you or worse still plough into the back of you, so it does get a bit nervy in the early part of most events. I picked my way through the early carnage with Dolores staying as close as possible to my back wheel as we headed out along the picturesque Hudson River to the north and the sunrise reveals the New York City skyline to the south. The course runs through the historic Pallisades, after the initial ten miles in northern New Jersey, you continue cycling north in New York State, along tree lined roads, rolling hills and fast descents, still skirting along the historic Hudson River. It was raining heavily and very misty. The first climb on the route was Alpine and as the very large peloton crested the summit the day began to clear up.

As you settle into this type of event after twenty miles or so you find your rhythm and usually a group that you get comfortable with riding along at the same pace. I had decided to stay with Dolores until the finish of the 50 mile route. Earnán and the others continued along the 100 mile route. We joined forces with a nice lively group as we started to climb Bear Mountain to the halfway marker of the entire course at the top. Dolores was chuffed to complete her cycle and wished me well for the remainder. After restocking at the feed station at the summit I pushed on for the final 50 miles. On the descent off Bear Mountain you can see the entire Hudson Valley, next up are several challenging climbs while winding through picturesque Rockland County back to the Palisades and up to the final climb to the finish line at Fort Lee. The entire finish village is alive with music, photos, podium ceremonies and a well- earned post – race meal. The drink stand, pasta party, bbq, beer and wine garden are open to cyclists, family and friends. Shower and washing facilities also provided. The second half of the day was brilliant, the sun came out and I really enjoyed the cycle. It felt good to chalk up another sporting achievement in New York. After spending a few hours around the finish village it was time to transfer bike and body back to the hotel and hit Time Square for a bite to eat and a celebratory few pints. We ended up in Connolly's - "a true Irish pub in the heart of time square". The food and staff were brilliant and the music and fantastic atmosphere made for a brilliant night of celebration after completing GFNY 2018.

On returning from a successful trip to the Big Apple, it was six months exactly to our Everest departure at the end of November, 2018. I rested for a week and let my body recuperate and my energy levels come back up again. The hiking and mountain training became more intensive, Seán and myself concentrated for a few weeks on carrying over twenty kgs in our backpacks to get used to the weight of the load we would be carrying on Everest and also get used to being able to balance correctly in all terrain while fully loaded. On Thursday June 28th we hopped on a flight to Glasgow for a few days of intensive training in the Scottish Highlands, on Ben Nevis and the famous Ring of Steal. Ben Nevis stands at 1,345 metres above sea level, the highest mountain in Scotland and the United Kingdom. Located deep in the north-western Scottish Highlands, towering over the town of Fort William. The name Ben Nevis is said to be from the old Scottish Gaelic "Bein Nibheis", meaning venomous mountain. This would match its fearsome reputation! The summit gets a lot of rain, snow and is constantly in cloud cover. For our visit in June 2018 the weather was brilliant. Temperatures soared to 25 degrees Celsius during our few days based in Fort William. We experienced epic views from the summit of Ben Nevis the surrounding mountain ranges and across the inner seas to Northern Ireland. It can take about four hours to summit and another two or three to get back down, depending on your fitness and the weather conditions. It is usually eight degrees colder at the top of Ben Nevis than at the base. At about 750 metres from the summit we went through some sections completely covered in snow, even though it was 25 degrees Celsius at the bottom. The descent can be tricky as it gets very slippery and some sections are steep and it can be difficult to maintain your balance. We managed the hike in six hours including a nice bit of lunch at the top and a chat with some fellow hikers. The following day we completed the Ring of Steal, the name given to the circular route in the heart of the Mamores range of mountains situated between Ben Nevis and Loch Leven. Starting and finishing in Glen Nevis, the route takes in some spectacular scenery, as you walk by the Falls of Steal, Scotland's second highest waterfall. The Ring of Steal gives a chance to complete six or seven Munros, four or five is more realistic in a day.

A Munro is a Scottish mountain with an elevation of more than 3,000 feet (914 metres). We bagged four Munros and it took us over nine hours from start to finish. The day was exhausting and extremely warm and we ran out of water and food as we had underestimated the challenge and the terrain. We took in An Gearanach, Stob Coire a'Chàirn, Am Bodach and the Devil's Ridge, each are linked by grassy crests and narrow rocky ridges. We were both knackered and starving on our return to Fort William. As is the case with most successful summits of any mountains we celebrated our fruitful training weekend in Fort William with a nice meal and a few scoops in the Nevis Inn. We have been to the Scottish Highlands on a few occasions with our own hiking group to train. Glencoe in particular offers vast mountain ranges as you trek along the Mamores mountain path, Cairngorm, Glen Nevis Valley at the foot of Ben Nevis, the setting for 'Braveheart' the award-winning Mel Gibson epic, the scenic beauty of the glen has led to its inclusion in the Ben Nevis and Glen Coe National Scenic areas. For winter training skills it's also ideal as it gets a large amount of snow and the Scottish Highlands take on a whole new disguise in the winter months, making the place a huge draw for climbers from all around the globe.

After our return from Fort William we made a plan for the remainder of our preparation time before our departure for Nepal. We varied our training, some long nine/ten hour walks on the flat mixed with hilly/mountainous ascents. We did Carrantuohill on a few occasions at 1,040 metres Ireland's highest peak. We spent weekends in Connemara on the Twelve Bens and regularly visited the Burren on my doorstep. Getting the recommended vaccines was the next thing to be completed, as some required a double dose a few weeks apart. These included. 1)Tetanus 2)Hepatitis A 3)Hepatitis B 4)Typhoid 5)Poliomyelitis 6)Rabies 7)Meningococcal Meningitis 8)Japanese Encephalitis 9)Yellow Fever –optional. My system reacted to the first shots, making me feel quite nauseous, sweaty and dehydrated. Seán did not have any such issues. While the travel companies make recommendations about which vaccines to get it is best to check through the Centres for Disease Control and Prevention CDC or your local Travel Medical Centre.

Thursday November 22nd, 2018 was a date that had been on the horizon for many months. There was still thirty nine days left in 2018. We were due to spend 15 of them on Mount Everest on the roof of the World. The packing

103

was done, the preparation complete, the body was in good (great) shape and the mind was ready. Flights with Emirates Airlines from Dublin to Dubaiat 20.50, a seven hour flight. Getting into Dubai on the morning of the 23rd of Nov. (3hrs ahead of Ireland). From Dubai we catch a connecting flight to Kathmandu the capital of Nepal getting in there at 18.00 local time (4hrs and 45mins ahead of Ireland). We got through security and the tourist visa application process fairly quickly. We had been warned that this process to acquire a visa can take many hours due to long queues at the Department of Immigration, but luckily we managed it quicker than expected. You can purchase your visa for 15 days -30 USD, 30 days - 50 USD, 90 days -125 USD. The airport is chaotic and very busy with long queues at security checks and baggage retrieval. All this can be overwhelming, so you need to keep your wits about you and take it all in your stride and accept it as part of the experience! We headed outside to our meeting point to join up with our guide. Ah sweet Jayzus! If inside the airport was mad, outside brought things to a different level entirely, it was crazy!! Overenthusiastic taxi drivers offering to take you to your hotel for a good price, porters looking to carry your luggage, giving you a trolley and bringing you to your taxi or green bus for public transport for tips. Huge crowds everywhere. It was clammy and the air tasted dusty and heavy. We hooked up with our guide carrying an Ian Taylor sign as planned. He brought us through the packed car park and introduced us to his brother (the driver). Our journey to the hotel was epic!! Seán and myself are plus 6ft. 1" and a bit. We were squashed into a small Suzuki with our luggage (two large duffle bags and two large rucksacks each) and the two brothers in the front. There are cars and cars and cars and more cars and small buses and motor bikes and motor bikes and motorbikes and trucks and trucks and bikes and bikes and pedestrians and more pedestrians on small tiny roads. There are no observed traffic laws in Kathmandu. Unless there are police at junctions directing traffic, it's everyone for themselves. No one let's anyone out and there is no right of way. All traffic coming together in one big jam with no apparent rules except that the first person to a space is entitled to it. It's total mayhem with drivers honking horns constantly and heading for gaps that don't exist. The traffic moves slow enough to allow for this sort of movement and it is strangely efficient. The dust and pollution were very evident on the drive from the airport. Kathmandu is ranked as one of the most polluted cities in the world. Mask wearing when outside especially is highly advisable. Our driver was able to negotiate this minefield of traffic while continuously texting with his left hand and at times his right hand on a small Nokia phone (we had them in Ireland twenty years ago).

We made it to our hotel the Yatri Suites and Spa in Thamel, which is in the main tourist district of the city, full of hotels, shops, bars and restaurants. Our itinerary included two nights at the Yatri Suites and two further nights after our safe return off Everest. After checking in we ventured out for dinner and a walk around. Small windy narrow streets full of stalls and small shops, bars and cafés and restaurants, tons of them. The streets of Kathmandu are chaotic and colourful with very few footpaths so you are walking on the roads trying to dodge traffic and other pedestrians. After dinner we found Paddy Foley's Irish bar – of course we did! It was hopping with music and a multi-cultural crowd of customers. We had a few beers and some chats with fellow hikers and mountaineers, some starting their expedition like ourselves and more who had completed theirs. Saturday was for rest and acclimatising to our new surroundings and getting over any jet lag. We had a team briefing at 5pm local time in the hotel. Here we met the other team members (eight in total) and some of our Sherpa's. Dawa was an elderly man with huge mountain experience, he did most of the talking and gave all the instructions and carefully went through our itinerary, answering any questions and making sure we were all comfortable with everything. While Dawa handles all the logistics in Kathmandu we were then introduced to our lead Sherpa for the expedition – Kalden Sherpa. A tall broad beast of a man with a lovely smile, who spoke very good English. He basically called all the shots, gave instructions to all the other Sherpas and was captain and manager of our group. He had completed and guided many expeditions to Everest Base camp, he was part of a team who had reached camp 4 heading to the summit of Everest on April 25th, 2015 when an avalanche triggered by an earthquake struck Mount Everest Base camp below, resulting in fifteen deaths and over seventy injuries. Kalden and the rest of the team had to descend back down to EBC and help with the rescue operations. In 2016 he was part of a team who had made it to the death zone but were driven back down the mountain by extremely bad weather. Kalden had successfully summated many 8,000 metre mountains. He briefed us on the formation and pace he wanted us to hike, gave us tips on hydration, food, breathing, what to carry with us in our rucksacks and the weather promised for the next day. They go day by day only, as the weather and conditions are so changeable, especially as we ascend. He will brief us every night after dinner when we get on the mountain. We are instructed to meet in the hotel lobby at 4.30am Sunday morning November 25th for transfer to the airport and a short flight to Lukla. After the briefing we headed off to a nice restaurant on Dawa's recommendation and a chance to get to know one another. Our team was made up of three Americans – Mary, Ronan and Kyle (Mary and Ronan are mother and son). A French man Sebestain (Seb) an English man Lee Robinson and three from Ireland - myself, Seán and Brian Conneely. Lee and Brian are based in the UAE working on construction projects and are good friends. Ironically Brian is from Clifden in Co. Galway only fifty miles from Carraroe our hometown. We had never met before this trip however. We all had a lovely relaxing evening getting to know one another over a meal and a few beers.

DAY 1 - Sunday morning November 25th, 2018 at 4.30am

The team meet in the Yatri Suites hotel lobby. After a small breakfast we shuffle outside with our baggage, which we had to pare back as much as possible due to weight restrictions on the flight to Tenzing Hilary Airport or Lukla airport. We could store whatever we did not require at the hotel until we returned. This is easier said than done. Seán and myself pondered long and hard the evening before on what we could afford to leave out, changing our minds regularly. Not easy when you are heading up close to the top of the world, you kind of need to have gear and clothing for all kinds of weather. As we waited for our minibus shuttle for the airport outside the hotel it was dark and cold, everyone was nervous and apprehensive. You could cut the tension as we made the short twenty minutes trip to catch our flight through the streets of Thamel and Kathmandu. After some negotiations regarding additional baggage weight, a payment was made and we were allowed to board the plane. Multiple flights carry hikers between Kathmandu and Lukla every day. Tenzing Hillary Airport, is named after Tenzing Norgay and Edmund Hillary, the first two people to climb Mount Everest. The airport sits at 2,859 metres and is surrounded on all sides by steep, mountainous terrain. The short runway is perched on little more than a mountain shelf. At one end there's a mountain face and at the other an enormous drop into the valley below. The thinner air at high altitude makes it more difficult for engines to create thrust for take-off. Meanwhile the reduced resistance also makes it harder to slow the plane down when landing. Lukla Airport runway is extremely short at 527metres, made out of paved asphalt sitting on a narrow mountain shelf. It is so short that it has a

12% uphill incline to assist planes in slowing down as they land. Due to the mountainous terrain, there are no go around procedures at the airport. This means that once a pilot has commenced an approach, they are committed to landing. So, it's land it or crash it! There are no radar or navigation systems, the pilots are completely and totally reliant on what they can see from the cockpit. Only helicopters and short take-off and landing turboprop planes are allowed operate to the airport. The other contributing factor that makes Lukla Airport the most dangerous in the world is the weather. Up to 50% of flights get cancelled. The weather in the Himalayas is extremely unpredictable. Flights from Kathmandu often turn around due to a sudden change in conditions at Lukla. Low visibility and crosswinds are the main culprits. The small mountain village settlement runway saw close to 130,000 passengers in 2019. In the last eighteen years it has claimed almost seventy lives and countless injured. Google Lukla Airport and have a look for yourself. The flight takes thirty five/forty minutes from Kathmandu. After a short bus ride from the terminal we got to our plane, a small twin otter aircraft looking a little rough around the edges. As I boarded a nice good-looking hostess told me to "Mind your head sir and have happy landings!" The weather was foggy and grey at first, but as we left the Kathmandu Valley, the clouds opened to blue skies and we started to relax into our scenic flight of the Everest region en route to Lukla, Nepal. These small planes are really basic and feel sort of slapped together, a bare – bones flight with no cabin service. Two rows of eight single seats on both sides. I was on the left side of the plane two rows back from the cockpit. Those of us on the left had the very best views as we made our way through and around the mountains. Sitting so close to the open cockpit I could see the pilot's instruments constantly flash "obstacle ahead" as we passed one massive mountain after another including our first glimpse of Everest. We hit a bit of turbulence but the pilot seemed cool as a cucumber. As I glimpsed over the cockpit window I saw a tiny landing strip like a handkerchief on the ground. Were we really going to land a plane there in the middle of the mountains? The pilot steadied the ship literally and went for it, in a few minutes we hit the runway and we were speeding towards the mountain face, he was on his 'a game' today and veered right and brought the plane to a stop. Everyone on board let out a roar and clapped hands. We had survived the famous flight to this crazy little airstrip dangling off the side of a mountain. I will admit I felt a bit giddy, not only for surviving flying to Lukla, but to be following in the footsteps of legendary adventurers on this famous mountain.

We retrieved our luggage and gathered outside the tiny airport. Kalden introduced us to the other Sherpas who would accompany us for the expedition. Prabesh, Arjin and Chongba. Ian Taylor trekking uses one Sherpa to every two hikers. Our larger duffle bags will be transported by four yaks and we will carry our twenty kgs rucksacks/ backpacks. The duffle bags would be collected early each day, we would leave them at a collection point and the yaks would ferry them to our next stop for the night. This means your backpack for the day needed to have anything you might require while hiking to the next destination. This includes essentials like water, food/ snacks, camera, headlamp, rain jacket and leggings, extra layers, sun protection, sun glasses, insect repellent, first aid kit, knife, woolly hat, peaked cap, sun hat, trekking poles, gloves, glove liners, buff or bandana, lip balm, dry bags, wipes, bog roll, hand sanitiser, anti-chafe cream, wipes, water filter or iodine purification tablets, solar charger/power bank. The duffle bag holds extra clothing, medicines, toiletries, footwear, sleeping bag, extra food, carbohydrate and protein bars, in short all the stuff you will need as the days click on. It's impossible to access the duffle bag during the day after the porters have picked it up until you arrive at your tea house in the evening. So, putting plenty of thought into the contents of your daypack is critical. The porter loads up the four yaks and heads away each morning early. We set off from Lukla for Monju. After a cold start the sun came out and it was crisp clear and ideal. Paths were very busy with yaks and mules and porters carrying all sorts of provisions. We also met many climbers descending back down. We covered fourteen kms today in just over six hours, not including a nice lunch stop at Phakding along the route. Terrain was hard as we hiked on stony paths and across steel rope bridges over beautiful white and blue watered rivers far below. A photographer's heaven. Our tea house or lodge for tonight at Monju is basic! Food is good however no bog roll, no towels, one tiny feint light in our little sleeping square/room and no bed clothes. Our first night in a sleeping bag and I really struggled to get in and out of it!! Before finishing up for the evening I tried to complete my media work. I had decided to write a blog on our progress. First day of actual hiking done and dusted, father and son felt good and looking forward to the rest of our adventure.

DAY 2 - Monday, November 26th, 2018

Breakfast at 7am for 8am departure. Today we gain another 800 metres in altitude on our way to Namche Bazaar. This morning the conversation at breakfast was about some furry friends who visited many rooms during the night. Seán and I had no such visitors, they must have heard us speaking in Irish! Today's hike was just over nine kms. Pleasant sunshine after a chilly start, every one of us started to feel the elevation gain and the conversation was a bit muted for that reason. Track was fairly steep in places and uneven underfoot. We cross some more beautiful suspension bridges as we gradually move uphill to the entrance to the Sagarmatha National Park, the official entrance to the Everest Region. The trail follows the river to the final high suspension bridge, after crossing here we begin the hike up "Namche Hill" which takes us nearly two hours before we reach the Sherpa village of Namche Bazaar. Today we hike slowly so we can adjust to the lower oxygen levels. This is our base for three nights at 3,350 metres. Our lodgings are decent with a toilet (not a flushing type) a hole in the floor job that you squat over. We also had a bit of a shower with very low pressure. The things we take for granted in our lives. The food here is also pretty good.

DAY 3 and DAY 4 - Namche Bazaar

For these two days we hike up a bit at a slow pace, trying to get our bodies to acclimatise and get used to the high altitude. In climbing speak we "climb high and sleep low" going a bit higher the second day and back down again. Ian Taylor strongly recommends three nights at Namche after doing a lot of research, they have found this is critical to success. Day 3 Tuesday, November 27th we head up to the Sherpa Museum, which holds a stunning view of Mount Everest and surrounding peaks. It takes us just under an hour to get up to the monastery and the viewing point, here we learn about Sagarmatha National Park, the Sherpa culture and the surrounding beautiful mountain region. Elevation gain today was only 200 metres, but the bodies are having to adjust to operating at this altitude and are being slowly introduced to it. We then spend the rest of the day relaxing, hydrating and enjoying the lovely unique Sherpa capital of Namche Bazaar, with its little shops and coffee and cake houses. Day 4 Wednesday, November 28th, another acclimatisation day. We hike up a very steep trail on the western side of Namche while walking on a steep stair way. We feel the lack of oxygen while we ascend 480 metres to Shangbouche Airstrip, a short grassy airstrip used by helicopters to drop supplies mainly. Here we cross the runway and head up Shangbouche Hill another 100 metres of altitude. We are now at 3,900 metres. Western Europeans are not used to operating at this altitude above sea level, so a slow gradual introduction is critical to avoid altitude related issues. After we enjoy the beautiful views in bright sunshine we descend down to Namche again after 4.5 hours. We enjoy lunch in the lodge and venture out for a slow ramble around, visiting some shops selling artefacts and climbing gear of all descriptions. We parked ourselves in one of a host of cafés and bakeries, enjoyed some coffee and beautiful cakes and pastries and chatted away to fellow hikers during the late afternoon. One such group of Polish climbers had just descended after making it to Base Camp. Most of their group of fifteen had been very sick with altitude sickness and diarrhoea. One had been air lifted to hospital by helicopter earlier today, other members were still on the descent and battling the effects. Two of the group were warning us of the extremes that lay ahead while also commenting on the beautiful unforgettable surroundings they had witnessed. The conversation brought home to the five members of our team sitting in the café eating cake and drinking coffee just what a serious expedition we are attempting and how powerful and challenging this mythical mountain is. We have had a relatively easy time so far. Tonight again in Namche for the fourth night on this mountain I am struggling to get into my sleeping bag. Because of trying to keep hydrated and drinking loads of fluids I get up to pee during the night and every time I get out and into my bag is a pain. During one of these occasions Seán is awake and he bursts out laughing. "What's so fucking funny"? I said. "You are," he said. "What do you mean"? "There is a wider adjustment on your bag and you have it on the tightest for much smaller people" Ah lads, he watched me struggle for three nights and didn't tell me!! You got me there Seán. When I closed it on the wider zip, it was like putting a big extension on a small kitchen. Thanks Sean, I will get you back have no doubt. At tonight's team briefing after dinner we are informed that from here to Base Camp and back to Namche again all toilet and shower facilities are communal if they exist at all, and some are outside toilets. No showers from here on. No drinking water not even on the toothbrush without treating it with purification tablets. No shaving, protect yourself from the extreme elements, no fruit without first peeling it, no meat as it can be in stock for months. Ease back on the coffee, causes dehydration. black tea with lemon, ginger and honey is highly recommended. Run a mile or two from anybody sneezing or coughing. Cover your mouth and nose while on the track. Plenty of sun cream as the sun can burn quickly up here. Layer up in the cold. Drink gallons of water and then another gallon. Save your energy as much as possible at altitude, don't walk too fast, don't step in the yak or mule shit.

DAY 5 - Namche Bazaar to Tengboche - twelve kilometres – Thursday, November 29th.

At 8am we kicked on for Tengboche at 3,900 metres after an early breakfast. Temperatures rose quickly and within an hour it was sixteen/eighteen degrees Celsius. The team are largely in good spirits if a little apprehensive. Staying healthy is the main concern, none of us have been to this altitude before and we don't know how the bodies will react. Most of the group have decided to take Diamox and have been on it since the start. This medication is effective in preventing acute mountain sickness (AMS), high altitude pulmonary oedema (HAPE), and high altitude cerebral oedema (HACE), dizziness and shortness of breath that can occur when you climb quickly to high altitude, generally above 3,050metres. One of the lads was taking Viagra and said it had similar benefits to Diamox! I had decided not to take Diamox at the beginning as I thought I would be able to cope with the altitude, and no I didn't take Viagra either. The previous night I suffered a bit of breathlessness and woke up with palpitations and a feeling of slight anxiety. These symptoms are associated with exposure to altitude. I decided to take a half tablet twice a day from this morning on. One of the side effects is being thirsty and needing to consume more water. Sometimes Diamox can cause light-headedness or dizziness and dry mouth. Our hiking time today was six hours to Tengboche. We got our first views of the Khumbu and brilliant views of Everest and the surrounding peaks, L'Hotse, Nuptse and Ama Dablam. Hugely significant peaks in mountaineering terms. Next we cross over the Dudh Kosi River, the highest river in Nepal in terms of elevation and continue up a very steep climb to Tengboche at 3,900 metres. We checked in to our lodge and then visited one of the most famous monasteries of Nepal. It's the leading Buddhist centre in the Khumbu region with a residing Rinpoche (a Tibetan spiritual leader) who blesses pilgrims and mountaineers passing through. Our tea house or lodge for tonight could be described as basic, but it's worse actually. Toilets are becoming more basic, plenty of squatting over a hole in the floor or ground, sleeping on a sheet of plywood in the sleeping bag, food is not even lukewarm as they have a problem with the solar power. After dinner we gather around a stove burning dried yak shit, it's what they use for fires. The women and children collect it fresh off the path each day, its dried gradually and stacked like a reek of turf to be used for the fire and to generate heat. We get to chat to another team, or what's left of them, descending back down from Base Camp. They started with nine and only three have survived. The rest had been evacuated with a mixture of acute mountain sickness (AMS) and some others got diarrhoea and food poisoning. It goes to show that anything can happen on this mountain. Tonight is really cold at minus ten and we resort to wearing some of our thermal clothing in the sleeping bag. I can hear the furry lads running around for most of the night, these lads are wearing boots I swear with the racket! We are told at tonight's briefing to expect really cold nights and mornings from now on, minus twenty to minus twenty five. It snowed hard at Base Camp today. Sean has been adopted by the Sherpas at this stage and he keeps reminding us, they are amazed at his strength, fitness and agility. Our team of eight are all still healthy and in good form.

DAY 6 - November 30th, Heading for Dingbouche at 4,410 metres – 13 kilometres.

Very cold start this morning, minus ten as the trail heads down-hill and continues very gradually up and down hills before crossing the river and uphill to Pangbouche where we have a tea break and then continue to Shomare for lunch. Pangbouche is home to many of the Sherpas who work on this imposing mountain each post monsoon season, so they can earn some money to help themselves and their families get through the harsh winters. The sun came out eventually and we experienced another surge in temperatures for a few hours as it got very warm. After lunch it's a gradual uphill trek towards the Imja Valley looking towards Island Peak. We pass some landslide areas on our left, as this location suffered most after recent earthquakes. Having completed six hours and fifteen minutes of trekking we arrive at our lodge at the top of the small town. We are based in Dingbouche for two nights for more acclimatising before we push higher to 5,000 metres. After dinner I continue to write up my blog in a quiet corner and then join the rest as we all snuggle around a stove in the middle of the room, listening to stories from other climbers and marvelling at their experiences. The communal loo is busy during the night and unfortunately Seán and myself are in a small room next door to it. Between the noise from people going in and out and the smells and the sounds from within (the walls are paper thin) neither of us get too much sleep! Some individuals are very noisy while using the facilities!

DAY 7 - Dingbouche - December 1st   Acclimatization day - 3kms.

Today we gain another 550 metres aiming to reach 4,900 metres. To you reading this, 550 metres may seem a very small gain, but it's huge at this altitude. We are pushing the acclimatisation process in preparation for moving even higher on the trail to Mount Everest. Twice every day at breakfast and after dinner before the team briefing we are all tested for Resting Heart Rate and Oxygen Saturation stats. Our readings have to be compared on two occasions daily to make sure we are remaining at the required levels. Any changes or alarm bells of any kind and you are evacuated without delay by helicopter. It takes us two hours to reach our destination and altitude. We relax here and take in the amazing views of Ama Dablam, Island Peak, Lhotse and the surrounding mountains. While we rest and relax at this height our bodies are adapting to the different demands of operating and even breathing at this level. We spend forty five minutes here and then we descend back down to Dingbouche again, where we spend the afternoon relaxing and re-hydrating. We have now been to an elevation of just under 5,000 metres. Our team is still intact and all seem well. One of the jobs to be completed every evening is preparing the backpack for the next day, depending on the weather that has been forecast to determine what extra clothing is required, preparing your water and food and snacks and recharging your phone and camera if possible. Early the next morning you finish packing the duffle bag before it's collected by the porter for transporting on board the yaks.

DAY 8 - Sunday, December 2nd, 2018. – My Birthday! Dingbouche to Lobouche at 4,950 metres.

We set off at 8am, it is stingingly cold, the sun did come out later but the temperature never really lifted all day, remaining around freezing and below. We made slow steady progress as our bodies adapted to the cold and extreme altitude. The trail heads towards the Khumbu Valley and continues on a long and slow trek across a beautiful, elevated route towards Tukla at

4,620 mtrs. We grab some soup and lunch here and rest for an hour. I actually had a small doze as we relaxed in the sunshine after lunch. We head away for Lobuche, getting over the Tukla pass. This is all uphill for an hour or so to reach the top of the pass. We then enter the Everest Memorial. We stop here to honour those that have lost their lives on this mythical mountain. Famous Sherpas and International climbers alike are remembered here. The dead are honoured with cairns, prayer flags and memorial monuments everywhere. I found it a very spiritual place, reading all the names of climbers that never returned from Everest. The Sherpas in our group were very respectful and went around and honoured the dead in their own way. Shortly after leaving the Everest Memorial we crossed the Kumbu River and saw at first hand the damage and destruction caused by the landslide that hit Base Camp after an earthquake in 2015. On the afternoon of April 25th 2015, Nepal and surrounding countries was struck by an earthquake. The shaking from the quake triggered an avalanche from Pumor into Base Camp killing at least twenty two people and injuring many more, surpassing an avalanche that occurred in 2014 as the deadliest disaster on the mountain. The quake caused a landslide pushing thousands of tons of stone and gravel down the mountain, leaving devastation in its wake. Today had not been a good day for one of our team. Kyle from Michigan USA was suffering with altitude sickness and was finding it really difficult to make any progress on the trail. This slowed us down a bit as the Sherpas tried and succeeded in getting Kyle to Lobouche. They will monitor him over night and make a decision in the morning on whether he continues to BC or has to be brought off the mountain. My birthday was celebrated at dinner tonight with lukewarm pasta and a cold potato on top with a candle stuck in it. They tried to mark the occasion in fairness. A problem with the solar power earlier meant cooking and heating food was impossible. This lodge for tonight was overcrowded, people were stretched everywhere, meaning the toilet and wash basin were really a no go area. It was minus twenty five in Lobouche. I got up at some hour to pee, I came up with a plan rather than marching down the corridor, I peed in a water bottle in our tiny room and fecked it into my sleeping bag as a hot water bottle, needs must they say! This became a ritual for me for a couple of nights at high altitude. Doing so in a very confined space without disturbing your companion can be difficult. It was still better than making your way in the freezing cold to a very unhygienic toilet. The hot water bottle helped heat up the toes! My roommate tells of how he had to listen to this procedure and how he hoped my bottle would hold the full deposit! In Dingboche the last two nights and again tonight in Lobouche we had to sleep in all our down jackets, thermal underwear hats gloves and socks, we also had to dump phones, cameras, chargers, garmin equipment and electrical goods into the bag to keep them out of the extreme cold. That's a great idea until you need to turn on your side during the night or get up to pee. Our breath was instantly freezing on the window in our tiny room. I was glad we were only spending one night in this hole. I will not forget that birthday in a hurry! In these conditions survival and coping mechanisms are of paramount importance. You are pushing and continuously testing your body, your psyche, your motivation and especially your mindset. You are constantly and consistently being challenged to overcome your fears and discomforts. At times nothing seems right. A cool head and attitude are gifts in these circumstances. Your goals and your visions are being questioned and tested. You must be strong minded, control your emotions, your effort, your tolerance levels and keep focused. I have found that if you allow one negative element of your situation to start to take up space in your mindset, it becomes a huge issue very quickly and it feeds other problems and issues and quickly takes over, like a snowball effect, getting bigger and bigger. My method of dealing with this is to acknowledge the situation or issue and ask myself can I change or improve it? If not, I accept it and remind myself it is temporary, even if temporary may be a long time. I change my focus on to myself again, what is positive and what needs to happen next to help me achieve my goal and guide me to my vision. In many instances you have to practice this again and again.

DAY 9 - Monday, December 3rd. - Lobouche to Gorakshep and on to Everest Base camp.

Kyle was assessed earlier and the Sherpas having spoken to him agree to let him keep going. He appears to have recovered a bit at least. The main difficulty when someone gets sick is trying to contain it. If it spreads, the rest of the group can be decimated very quickly. We head away from Lobouche after an early 6am breakfast, which this morning consisted of an omelette (with eggshells) two slices of toast and lemon, ginger and honey tea. I have become great friends with this type of black tea on our trip. It's nice and cooling for a dry throat from all the dust on the trail, it is also a booster for the immune system. Honey is great for the induced cough we all seem to have (the Khumbu cough as it is known, Khumbu with reference to the valley that leads up to Mount Everest). The cough is caused by the low humidity and temperatures associated with high altitudes. Ginger is also good for coughs and muscle pain, lemon is antibacterial and full of Vitamin C. Lemon, ginger and honey tea is a great natural boost for the immune system. Today is broken into two parts, firstly we get to Gorakshep after roughly three hours, have lunch and then we push on for Everest Base Camp for an additional two hours, then we come back to Gorakshep where we spend the night. Today's trek is beautiful and unique, we cross a lot of loose boulder fields and glacial moraine, left behind by a moving glacier. The trail goes up and down and is challenging all the way until we get to the Yeti Lodge at Gorakshep at 5,140 metres. After lunch we lightened our load at the lodge where we were to spend another sub-zero night, and then we pushed on for the round-trip to get to Base Camp. The terrain is mostly sandy as we leave Gorakshep becoming very rocky as we are now on the outskirts of the Khumbu Glacier. The gradient is moderate all the way but not steep and we are afforded great views of Mount Everest. Due to the massive landslides from 2015 we negotiate over boulders and rocks as the trail turns inwards. Just over two hours later we reach Base Camp at 5,364 metres. I am instantly overcome by emotion. We hug and high five each other and the other team members and of course the Sherpas. I look around and take stock of my surroundings, the aura about this place. The springboard for many summit attempts, the scene for all those Everest films, the place where so many perished and were seriously injured in 2015. EBC is marked with piles of stones, dozens of strings of prayer flags and a few "Everest Base Camp" signs also giving the elevation at this iconic spot. You cannot see Mount Everest from EBC, as there are other insanely tall mountains blocking the view. After taking some photos and relaxing in this famous place it was time to get back down to Gorakshep. It took us another two hours to get back, making it a long day of seven hours of trekking. At dinner tonight we are given the option of hiking up Kala Patthar at 5,645 metres to get the best views and see the sun rise over Mount Everest. Departure is at 4am. Five of our team opted to go for it. I got into my sleeping bag at 9pm having completed my blog for the last forty eight hours. I was not feeling 100% at dinner. I didn't sleep a wink, it was baltic, the temperature dropped to minus twenty six. But that was not the reason. I did not feel right. One minute I felt hot and sweaty and the next cold and gasping for air. Altitude sickness was kicking in! I had a really tough night and wasn't sure if I would be capable of climbing higher and gaining more altitude in a few hours.

DAY 10 - Tuesday, December 4th - 4am start up Kala Patthar at 5,645mtrs, then back to Gorakshep and depart after breakfast for Pheriche.

I got myself out of the sleeping bag at 3.30am and struggled to close the laces in my boots. I made it down the stairs where the others were waiting and supping mugs of lemon, ginger and honey and eating toast. Seán was encouraging me as he had done in the room earlier. I drank some tea but couldn't handle any toast as it was cold and hard. I took two bites out of an energy bar in my pocket. We did not need much in our backpacks so I was not carrying much weight, which was a help. We had two hours of hiking ahead to the summit of Kala Patthar. We set off at 4.10am into the darkness. The climb kicked up straight away and was really steep. I was literally in bits, I had no power and my breathing and heart rate were all over the place and erratic. As we were all wearing head torches no one could see me struggling. We were climbing in a single line formation following Keldan who was leading us. But I soon began to fall back and I could not stick with the slow pace he was setting. Seán realised I was in trouble and came back down to encourage me, (he actually did this on three occasions) offering food, water and support. He had never seen his father in this vulnerable state before, so his encouragement was much appreciated. I took some water off him as I could not access my own. The mouthpiece in my Camel Bac was frozen solid and the contents in my water bottle was also like a big ice cube. The temperature on my garmin watch read minus 27 degrees. Somehow for the next two hours I battled on and dragged my not so small frame to the summit of Kala Patthar. My thinking was strong and clear. I knew what was required and how I needed to do it. My body on the other hand didn't seem to be in sync with my brain and every move was slow and lethargic and took huge effort. As I arrived at the tight summit point, I made eye contact with Seán, he smiled and winked at me, we had an unspoken moment as our eyes met. I think he said to himself I knew you'd make it! The sunrise views over Mount Everest and the surrounding peaks were amazing and we marvelled at our location and the peace and tranquillity all around us at 6.15am. After some photos and a short rest we turned around and headed back to Gorakshep below. I began to improve very quickly as we dropped down in altitude, with literally every step I seemed to be breathing easier and my brain and body had re-aligned. Seán and two of the Sherpas decided to race back down to the lodge. He finished second. We packed up our duffle bags and sent them off, got our backpacks ready for the eight hour trek to Pheriche at 4,370 mtrs. My stomach was slow to settle and I didn't have much of a breakfast before departure, except for a protein bar and tea. I spoke to Kalden our lead Sherpa about my woes during the night and this morning. He smiled and said "this is Gorakshep Martin, nobody has good sleep and sometimes bad feelings too", - so there you go, shake yourself down Máirtín Óg and get on with it! As we descended during the morning my system settled down more and I improved considerably. For anyone who has completed multi day endurance events you know you are always going to have a bad day. (at least one). Today (day 10) was mine. During a one-day event unless you break a bone or pull a muscle you will usually make it to the finish. A multi day challenge is a different story especially on this monster of a mountain. If something goes wrong up here, if you break down on Everest in any way, it's curtains, game over, Call a "chopper" quick. Every single day you hear the constant chuf chuf of helicopters overhead. The Sherpas can determine by their flight path whether it is a medical emergency evacuation or a sightseeing flight. Most "Choppers" are for medical emergencies. There seemed to be one hundred of them in the sky today over us. I have to stop thinking like this and just concentrate on our trail down from this high altitude. Next crisis for me today came when the soles of my feet began to start burning up and get really sore. I wasn't sure was it tendonitis or plantar fasciitis, but it was fucking sore! I was physically in the best shape possible, but the last twelve/fourteen hours was really testing my resolve, mentally and psychologically. I swallowed a few pain killers and an anti-inflammatory and pushed on. After another hour the medication kicked in and I enjoyed the last few kilometres of the day in to Pheriche. We had descended down to 4,370 mtrs and all the team were tired but in good spirits. Tonight we stay in a nice clean lodge, with good food and we have the place to ourselves. I was tired this evening, it has been a very difficult twenty or so hours for me and I feel it in every part of my body. I have not showered in six days and I have ten day explorer facial growth which does nothing for my general appearance. I need to sleep and recuperate. Seán and Brian went off to another lodge near us to visit a Canadian crew (of women) they had become friendly with as we sporadically met along the way to EBC.

DAY 11 - Wednesday December 5th - Phericheto Namche Bazaar distance 23kms – 9hrs.

A long day ahead as we pull out of Pheriche. I slept well apart from one pee in the bottle during the night, I didn't even hear Seán come in. There is an initial uphill out of Pheriche, and then downhill as we pass Shomare and Pangbouche and a further one hour down to the riverside for lunch. Then we hike up through the forest for another hour and thirty minutes to reach Ama Dablam view lodge. From here we traverse around the mountainside and drop down into Namche Bazaar. Today as we drop down in levels of altitude we are moving at a high pace and we cover ground quickly. Namche is like a little oasis on the mountain. We enjoy a shower and a flushing toilet in our room this time and bed clothes. After a lovely meal we venture to the Irish Bar (even on the highest mountain in the world)! We enjoy playing pool here and celebrating with our Sherpas, they love to play pool and drink beer. They don't have the same capacity for it as western Europeans and they were hilariously funny after a few. It's nice to relax this evening, the stress has lifted considerably. Just get back to Lukla now and the flight back to Kathmandu Airport. Oh yes Lukla airport and that flight!

DAY 12 - Thursday December 6th - Namche Bazaar to Lukla – Distance 22kms - 8/9hrs.

Early start at 7am after a lovely breakfast of eggs and bread. Another long day in store and some of the team are feeling tired after so many days of multi-day hiking on challenging terrain. We start down Namche Hill and then across the Hillary Bridge and then long stretches of up and down all the way to Lukla. Kalden and the Sherpas are setting a lively pace, the sun is out early and it is becoming very warm. 20 degrees celsius. We exit the Sagarmartha National Park, pass through Monjo and Pkakding before we finally start the last steep uphill section to Lukla. We have one final night sleeping on the mountain. Our lodge for our last night is very basic and the opposite of neat, clean and tidy. It is right beside the airport and we notice a plane half way down the short runway, kind of nosed in to the side with a pool of oil clearly visible underneath it!?? We are informed that the plane had hydraulic brake failure before take-off! Lukla Airport does not disappoint. There is also an issue with the solar power in our lodge when we arrive. So that means no shower and no food! Lovely stuff! I have a wipes bath again, change my clothes, get out of the hiking boots for the last time and into my lighter trail shoes. We stroll into the small town perched at 2,860 metres on the side of a mountain. Lukla is most famous for being home to the most dangerous airstrip in the world. With so many tourists passing through every year the town has expanded and now has a variety of shops and small hotels and a couple of small bars. We find one such establishment and forge a relationship with the English speaking owner. Beers and food soon appear and we end the day on a real high having completed our hiking from Lukla to Everest Base Camp and back. We pack up most of our gear for the morning, before going to sleep in our sleeping bags again for the last time we hope.

DAY 13 - Friday December 7th - Fly Lukla Airport to Kathmandu 6.00am

Solar power has returned and we receive a warm breakfast, omelette and toast for me and my favourite lemon ginger and honey tea of course. A well-earned rest for the legs today as we walk the ten minutes to the small terminal. It's really busy and as we chat to other commuters we hear that only two flights out of six from Kathmandu had landed in Lukla so far due to heavy fog in Kathmandu. This caused a backlog, but the flights have now restarted. We will be delayed for only an hour and a half (hopefully) The small airport is not a very stimulating place by any means to spend a few hours but we make the best of it. Finally as more flights start to land and take off again, we get the call to board. As our plane speeds down the runway for take-off I can see flashing lights in the cockpit saying "abort abort" the Pilot ignores them and three minutes later we are climbing steeply around the mountains. After thirty five minutes we drop out of the clouds and start our descent into Kathmandu. As we hit the runway and landed safely, I felt my stomach head and body let out a sigh from within. We were off Everest and back to civilisation. The transfer back to The Yetti Suites Hotel was enjoyable. The hot shower and the next few hours sleep in a comfortable bed even sweeter. A celebration dinner was organised for us in a lovely restaurant by Dawa. After a good rest and a bit of shopping in the early evening, we headed to the restaurant and experienced a wonderful evening courtesy of our Sherpas. They presented us with some lovely gifts in honour of the achievement. Seán was presented with a special scarf and accepted as honorary Sherpa. We ventured back to Paddy Foley's Bar and finished off the night in high spirits. After a brilliant nights sleep we wandered around Kathmandu and it's amazing colourful streets on Saturday December 8th. We had a few coffees and some lunch with the Canadian girls and really appreciated what we had achieved. Most of our team had departed for early flights. Seán and I had an evening departure. As we headed for the airport at 7pm and our homebound flights, I said to myself that I will return to Nepal again soon.

Chapter 7 Summary

MOUNT EVEREST

My trip and expedition to Nepal - the Himalayas and Mount Everest was a really special event. A once in a lifetime opportunity, made all the more unique by the fact I was able to do it with Seán. I am extremely proud of our joint achievement. But I am especially proud of a hugely capable young man who is my son. To witness him perform so well in these exceedingly difficult surroundings and conditions was such a pleasure for me. Fair play Seán - you will go on to conquer many more challenges I have no doubt.

Personally, I found Nepal and the Himalayas very spiritual and emotional at times. Everest like all high-altitude mountains affords you space to think, to switch off or to switch on. You escape in the romance of the mountain, everything else is insignificant. It's you against the mountain. You are pushing your body, your psyche, your mindset and your motivation to the extreme. Everything else is shut away. Up here in the clouds it doesn't count. I found myself digging deep inside, to my guts, in the pit of my stomach to summon the energy to keep going to keep moving forward. At times I felt absorbed by the mountain, by the elements, the sun, the extreme cold, the frost, the slopes, the night time, the moon, the stars, the absolute silence, the beauty, the aura and the history of the mystical and mythical surroundings. When we rested my mind wandered and although I was extremely tired some nights, I felt energised deep inside. I felt extremely motivated and passionate.

I went through a process in my mind. I started to park all the stuff from my past. It was done and dusted. I became really aware of the present moment and my surroundings. My inner thoughts became positive and my emotions were joyous. I really appreciated being free from distractions and artificial and societal pressures, the stuff we put ourselves through on a daily basis. I felt connected to Mother Nature. It made me hit the brakes and realise that there is so much more to life. The Himalayas touched me deeply, the mountain range that separates Nepal and China. Home to some of the highest peaks on the globe (nine of the earth's ten highest). I loved seeing the children smile at us as we passed through the tiny mountain side villages as they played with cardboard boxes and pieces of string. The daily life of the people in the Khumbu Valley, I appreciated and absorbed the sights and scents of traditional Nepalese life. Stopping in tea houses and enjoying a warm welcome. Watching and experiencing the Sherpas at work. They work tirelessly and selflessly on the mountains carrying luggage and supplies and looking after clients and never seem to tire or get affected by the altitude. Loving to share a joke and always with a smile on their faces. Forces of nature as they are referred too. I felt an incredible connection with the mountains and I was astonished by their enormity. I loved the buzz from the vibrant Nepalese culture and the spiritual and kind nature of the people. I became so aware of the stressful manner in which we live our lives in the western world. The constant battles we fight trying to improve our lot, the emphasis we place on material things, not recognising and putting enough value on what really matters. I had started to look at my life and the way I was living it long before my trip to Nepal. Having had the experience now I feel an awakening within, a spiritual feeling and appreciation of commitment and working towards attaining a better balance and improving my understanding of myself and my contribution to others. I look forward to my return in the near future.

"Your vision will become clear only when you can look into your own heart. Who looks outside dreams, who looks inside, awakes."
- Carl Jung – Swiss psychiatrist and psychoanalyst.

Chapter 8

WHERE OTHERS FAILED I MADE A STAND

I found a strength deep inside that helped me reinvent myself again.

"If you really want to do something, you'll find a way.
If you don't, you'll find an excuse. – Jim Rohan

When the initial tremors of the financial crisis in March 2008 began to hit Ireland, it took a while before we realised what was really happening. On St. Patrick's Day 2008 stock markets around the world tumbled including the ISEQ index in Dublin. The share price of Anglo Irish Bank had collapsed in what became known as the 'St. Patrick's Day massacre'. The Celtic Tiger was coming to a shuddering halt. In the spring of 2008 there was talk of a recession in the air, largely due to over borrowing.

Property and land prices had already started to tumble. Senior government officials were reportedly saying the country is fucked. The ship of the state was sinking faster than the Titanic had. The banks were collapsing. By September, the Irish Government made a decision to guarantee the banking system. This turned out to be disastrous. US Banks-Lehman Brothers, Bear Stearns, JP Morgan are also in trouble.

In the UK, Northern Rock is nationalised by the government. This was a global crisis. I was caught up in this crisis and it was to leave an ever-lasting impression. Two of my favourite movies of the last fifteen or so years are – 'Everest' based on a true story. The 1996 Mount Everest disaster on May 10th, during which eight people died due to a blizzard while making summit attempts or trying to descend having already summitted. The movie focuses on the survival attempts of two expedition teams. One led by Rob Hall (Adventure Consultants Team) and the other by Scott Fischer (Mountain Madness Team). Life threatening high-altitude storms in the Himalayas are not unusual and hugely contribute to the difficulty of getting up and down the mountain safely and is recognised as a significant risk. Although there were many contributing factors on that day, some inexperienced climbers, no fixed ropes were set, climbers continued after the turnaround time, and some suffered from fatigue and altitude sickness. The major contributing factor to the disaster and loss of life was the continuing raging blizzard, making everyone vulnerable as oxygen supplies ran out.

The high-impact weather trapped twenty climbers on the exposed upper slopes of Mount Everest leading to the death of eight climbers. The experts maintain that the falling barometric pressure and the presence of ozone-rich stratospheric air that occurred near the summit during this event could have shifted a coping climber from a state of brittle tolerance to physiological distress.

Another of my other favourite movies –'The Perfect Storm' is also based on a true story. The 'Andrea Gail' a twelve year old, seventy foot vessel was scheduled to return to Gloucester, America's oldest seaport after a sword fishing trip to Newfoundland's Grand Banks, more than 900 miles away. The boat was carrying six crew members. Depending on the conditions and the amount of catch, the boats are usually out at sea for a month. The storm with no name claimed the lives of the six fishermen and the captain and crew of the 'Andrea Gail'.

The perfect storm in 1991 left a trail of destruction from Nova Scotia to Florida, killing thirteen people and causing close to $500 million in damage as it lashed the coast from Oct.26 to Nov.1st of that year. Winds upwards of 70 mph tossed boats in the harbours and lifted homes from their foundations. But days before the storm wreaked havoc on the East Coast, it was raging in the ocean with winds up to 120mph and the six men onboard Gloucester's 'Andrea Gail' found themselves right in the eye of the storm with no place to go!

Have you ever had the experience of being in similar circumstances or situations? Many people struggle with change and challenges. They do not cope well with having to adapt to doing things differently. Creatures of habit don't like the discomfort of the unknown. Nothing is guaranteed in this life and no one has a magic formula. Action is the common denominator that attempts to solve every difficulty in life and can also make dreams come true. There are so many people out there who are dealing with difficulties, with life, and without some motivation and inspiration, they'll go off the courses of their lives. The size of your problems or issues are different to everyone else, but hugely relevant to you. Whether its business, career or personal it can be really challenging to come up with creative solutions to the issues.

My personal 'Everest' or my 'Perfect Storm' deeply affected every part of my own life and that of my family. The financial crisis and the resultant fall out had left me stranded on the perilous exposed slopes of my entire life. My boat was caught up in the midst of a critical situation created by a powerful concurrence of factors. It felt more like death and very little like life! Taking action in critical scenarios when your energy levels are low and you are hostage to high levels of stress, worry and anxiety is near impossible. It takes huge strength of mind and character to push through these feelings and emotions. My confidence was gone completely, like a top class athlete or sports person who could no longer perform at the highest level. I could not find comfort from any source or in any place. I wanted to hide and to bury myself so deep that I wouldn't feel the anguish and hurt. Leaving my sisters small apartment every day and trying to function to some degree was very demanding.

I had no energy or drive, my willpower was at an all-time low. I seemed to be pulling a massive load around with me all the time. I could not escape it. The feeling never seemed to ease no matter what I was doing. It was like the worst form of grief. That physical pain and the racing mind. The only feelings I had were bad feelings, sadness and fear and anger and upset and loss. Stress and anxiety became a constant part of me, unable to sleep staring at the ceiling at all hours of the morning anxious about my problems. I was really struggling with my mental and emotional health and would discover a few years later the effect it had on my physical health.

As I mentioned in chapter five my sister Angela convinced me to go to a Life Coach, she firmly believed it would benefit me. A few days after our phone conversation I decided to make an appointment. When I went to my coach I was in a place of huge life transition. I had no clear vision. My confidence was gone and I felt overwhelmed. I had no idea what to expect. My only understanding of a coach was a sports coach and I was one of them myself. I coached Carraroe GAA teams, helping players improve their skills and developing tactics and I would also work on their mindset and motivation and commitment. I felt nervous when I met Lorna Mc Dowell upstairs in her cool office/workspace on the Tuam Road in Galway. It was weird meeting a total stranger to share my issues and thoughts with for the first time. I had no idea that the time I spent with Lorna would change my life so much. We had a bit of small talk before officially starting the session, she felt friendly and warm. She thanked me for reaching out and we got started. The ratio of our conversation was about 80% me and 20% Lorna. We dug deep into my situation. My business, my youth, my marriage, my family and my past times and passions. After ninety minutes at the end of the first session we discussed working together twice a week for the next three months. I was so whacked after that initial coaching session and this would become a pattern as we began to slowly work through my situation over time. I wasn't being judged or criticised. Lorna was supportive and actively listening to me and we worked on my goals and gaining more clarity. I accepted where I was and started to make small positive changes and only dealing with one or two small problems at a time. I was discovering significant breakthroughs about myself and I went away from most sessions tired but with my mind clear. It was great to talk to someone who was constructively helping me move from where I was. In modern day society you can learn anything online or from social media. You can learn cooking or learn how to do squats or dead lifts from watching videos. You can go through life doing your own thing and arguably improve on your own. But you can imagine how much more effective your learning will be if a chef taught you first hand. That has been my experience working with a Life Coach. I was paying for this of course and every time I came to a session I wanted to show I was making progress, my professional coach held me accountable and supported and motivated me. I quickly learned that I could do all of this on my own, she helped me with my transformation and accelerated my growth.

After a couple of weeks of Life Coaching and intentional effort I began to see changes in my behaviour mindset and beliefs. I was also enjoying the outdoors again. Meandering walks along the seashore and hearing the rippling waves gently lap against the shore or sending spray and white water up in the air gave me hope. I found the sound of the waves relaxing, washing away my cares and tension. Closing my eyes and concentrating on the waves crashing and tumbling through the pebbles was my form of meditation, helping me to unwind and wash away my cares and tensions. It was therapeutic and non-judgemental and never the same any day. For me, when I closed my eyes and listened, it felt like a soft comfortable massage where the waves were caressing my whole body and my mind, easing away my pain and soothing my deep throbbing wounds.

In the beginning the tears flowed in bucket loads but gradually after a few weeks they stopped and the experience became much more pleasurable and fulfilling. I began to understand that the only person who could save me was myself. I had no one else. Understanding that you are responsible for the welfare of your own life, and if things are going to change and be the way you want them to be, it depends on you. When you realise this, it is like a 'superpower' to get you through every obstacle life can throw at you. By all means seeking support is paramount and will help immensely, but ultimately you are your own saviour. Coaching helped me find peace with where I was and with that came acceptance. That brought calmness. Then I focused on self-respect and doing stuff that made me feel good. The process was slow and gradual.

Getting out of difficulties requires actions and therefore the need to make decisions. I made decisions to get out of my difficulties. I needed to firstly accept where I was and next begin to take action and not give in to doubts or fear. I could not receive advice from others as I knew no one who had been in similar situations. I used my inner gut, my intuition as my compass to guide me through. I slowed down the process to something manageable for myself and found making even the smallest of changes very rewarding. I had no solid ground under me to stabilise my fears and worries, I had nothing to hold on to so I could ease the pain or the fear, no scapegoat to blame, no one to shoulder some of the responsibility. It was my struggle and enormous pain that I was attempting to overcome my own Everest and my own Perfect Storm.

I could not force my transformation. I didn't know where I was headed or how to get there. I didn't know who I was. I lost my identity. My ego was trying to attach me to who I had been up to this point and to get back doing what I had been doing for most of my adult life. I desperately needed the approval of others, to be liked and praised and respected and appreciated. My ego wanted me to be involved in projects and trucks and machinery and I wanted to be a father and a friend and a person who made a positive difference in people's lives. But hold on a minute, I did not have that choice now to be or do any of those things. It had been taken away from me. I was in the eye of the storm, in the death zone near the summit of the mountain. This was about survival, not about the past or how I got here. I had to think beyond the present and find my path to the future. Navigate my way out of my present circumstances and remove any attachments to my ego and start on my new journey. I had another choice of course, go down with the ship, perish on the mountain!

In every chapter in this book there is a common thread, a golden thread or a recurring characteristic present in many events. That strong flame that burns within me, that inspires me to stay going.

In my darkest hour and weakest moments it still flickers and keeps me going. You have it too, I believe everyone does. I have had cause to look for it and find it many times in my life. Resilience empowers people to accept and adapt to situations and move forward. It's typically defined as the capacity to recover from difficult life events. It's your ability to withstand adversity and bounce back and grow despite life's problems. Resilience is not a fixed trait. Flexibility, adaptability and perseverance can help you tap into your resilience by changing certain thoughts and behaviours. According to Dr. Sood, a member of the Everyday Health Wellness Advisory Board, resilience can be defined in terms of five principles: Gratitude – Compassion – Acceptance – Meaning – Forgiveness. Resilience is what gives you the emotional strength to cope with trauma, adversity and hardship. Resilient people utilise their resources, strengths and skills to overcome challenges and work through setbacks. Dr Sood says resilience is "the core strength you use to lift the load of life."

It can also be broken down into categories or types: Psychological resilience – Emotional resilience – Physical resilience – Community resilience. I have faced personal crisis, illness, financial ruin, loss of loved ones and business wipe-out. I have taken on and accomplished extreme sporting challenges and all kinds of life experiences. I have adapted to adversity and change, loss and risk by demonstrating resilience while working through emotional pain and suffering.

My transformation was helped and aided by my Life Coach Lorna and, in no small way, by Dolores Sheehy my partner. I had worked on the eight day International Cycle Race around Ireland – the 'Rás' for many years as an official, in my role as a Commissaire driver.- French word for cycling race referee. I had stepped away for a couple of years with all I had going on! I was keeping a low profile and keeping to myself trying to come to terms with my situation and all that had transpired. I was summoned back again. The organisation needed someone with my experience as a Commissaire driver. Basically, I drove in amongst one hundred and eighty cyclists, thirty motor bike marshals and twenty team cars. High octane stuff. I enjoyed the buzz of it, for someone very interested in cycling it was like having a ring side seat at the biggest cycling event in the country. I was eventually persuaded to go back on the 'Rás'. That is when I met Dolores my partner. She eventually became the final and most important piece of my transformation, recovery and later my re-invention.

I spent a few years commuting to Dublin at weekends. The plant and machinery business was well and truly gone at this stage. I was trying to deal with the property and development stuff and especially the project at home in Carraroe. As you can imagine, this was proving really difficult for me. I would usually leave Dublin on Sunday night heading for Galway and spend the week sorting out issues, meeting clients and so on. This was having a really negative effect on my mental health. I could sense the energy draining out of me as soon as I got back to Galway thinking about the week ahead. AIB was putting me under enormous pressure to sell the remaining units and to also increase the rent roll. I had no income at this stage apart from selling off a few small items of builder's plant and rent from a small commercial unit.

I happened to meet a past business associate in a coffee shop in Galway one morning and we had a good conversation. This particular individual was in the same place and having the same difficulties as I was,, especially with the banks. It was the most meaningful and rewarding conversation I had in a long time. Even though this man did not lighten my load or take away my pain, it was strangely refreshing to talk to a person going through a similar experience. He highly recommended I make contact with a particular solicitor to help and advise me. I made an appointment for the following day at 3pm.Michael Mc Darby sat in his large office behind a brown desk with a black leather surface. He listened intently as I shared my story and he spoke only to question me about certain dates, figures and agreements. After just over sixty minutes the consultation finished and Michael agreed to help me. "Set up a meeting with your main bank a.s.a.p. and I will see you there," he said.

That meeting took place two weeks later in Galway with three bank officials. Michael and I were due to meet one hour beforehand to discuss tactics, he was late arriving as his previous engagement had run over. This did nothing for my shaky confidence about what lay ahead. "Don't open your mouth at the meeting and only speak if and when I ask you to do so," he said. We were ushered into a small office with four chairs and a glass table for the meeting. It was expected that I would be on my own as normal and another chair was hastily provided with an air of discomfort filling the small space with glass panels and a narrow glass door. The meeting got underway and as per usual the pressure dials were being turned up and pointed at me. I went to speak and respond and had barely opened my mouth when I felt the distinct pressure of a foot pressing hard on my toes. Michael purposely stood on my right foot as he got up from his chair and stood up with much force, knocking his chair back onto the floor with a bang. A formidable man with a white beard, he launched into a strong verbal speech after firstly dropping a pile of files from his arms onto the small glass table causing a loud clatter. The three bank officials were totally taken aback with this and his approach and it had the effect of turning up the uncomfortable stakes in the small room even more. Oh man, this had such a positive impact on me apart from my sore toes! At all the previous meetings and there had been many, I had felt alone on the mountain in gale force winds, or like a boxer in the ring trying to fight an army. This time I had help, shelter, someone in my corner. Sure, Michael was facing the wind with me, he had jumped into the ring beside me. He declared that he would not tolerate any longer the way I was being treated and abused. I had been co-operating up until then and I deserved some respect going forward or I would no longer play ball he informed the bankers. Then he instructed me to leave the meeting with him. The response he got was a limp "You can't do that and you can't behave like that," but he just replied "Contact my office if you are willing to engage with us and not Máirtín going forward," and off out the door we went. I could have kissed him! As we parted outside Michael assured me the bank would be back and "We will structure this in a different way for you". "What was in the big pile of files you dropped onto the table?" I asked. "Just a collection of files from other bigger cases I am involved with", he said.

Two weeks later we were at another meeting with the bank in a much bigger office this time, where Michael negotiated a different deal for me to stay involved with the project, help get clients across the line and sell the last number of units. He made sure with the banks blessing that I would receive part of the existing rent roll to cover my costs (and keep me afloat) and a percentage of the sale agreed price on any units sold going forward. This was massive for me at this time and relieved a lot of my stress and provided me with a little comfort around my income. Michael's approach was completely different, he banged a few more desks and doors, he stood up for me and put a stop to the pressure and abuse and instigated the early part of an eventual settlement or deal with the bank. There is a major life lesson in this. No one in any situation should have to put up with abuse or mental pressure. Stand up and speak up for yourself, or seek help from a professional person, change your situation or your job or career if you need too. Don't live under this type of stress under any circumstances. Mr. Mc Darby never charged me for his services! He called it a gentleman's agreement to be dealt with in the future.

Dolores convinced me to move to Dublin permanently as our relationship developed. It was like a new lease of life for me when I eventually did. I still had to come to Galway and Carraroe a few times a month to clear up stuff and meet clients etc, but I kept the visits to a minimum and tried to get a couple of appointments together in the same day when I could. It was still having a negative effect on me, I tried to be positive in my dealings with others but the negative energy within me around the whole situation was debilitating. Shortly after moving to Dublin I got shingles again. This was my third dose. Medication was successful on the first occasion but not the second time. Shingles is triggered by a weakened or compromised immune system. It's a viral infection that causes painful rashes on your torso and also triggers painful acute nerve pain. I had been dealing with chronic stress for a prolonged period of time and my immune system was weakened and struggling to cope and screaming for mercy at the same time! I did not get any rash this third occasion, just spots on my chest and stomach, but the sudden jolts of severe nerve pain were excruciating, like being stabbed with a knife and making me feel sick in my stomach. Holding my breath and not moving a muscle was the only thing I could do until the severe pain passed away. On the worst days I was getting these jolts five or six times every hour. I was totally flattened by this virus for seven weeks. Little did I realise how much of a signal this was from my body for what was to come at a later stage. This was literally killing me. I had to try and disassociate myself from my problems and leave them behind as much as I could. I had to stay away from the stress I was dealing with and feeling.

Dolores encouraged me to try different things. I started cooking and baking. I had never done much of it before. Baking brown bread and fresh scones became second nature. I was pushing the boat out with the dinners after initially perfecting a roast chicken or lamb or roast beef and gravy, I graduated myself on to chicken tikka masala and meatballs and homemade pizzas. I experimented with various fish and my salads took on a Mediterranean feel! Thanks to Jamie Oliver, my omelettes and Mexican breakfast became my signature dishes. I set a vegetable and potato plot in the back garden in the estate in Clonsilla where we lived. Being creative and realising I had other talents I could develop was brilliant for my self-esteem and confidence. Planting seeds in the back garden of a housing estate in North Dublin is not common practice, but I loved the results of my efforts. Walking out with a spade and harvesting my own potatoes and having my own cabbage, carrots onions, peas, cucumbers, lettuce and so on felt invigorating. Preparing nice wholesome food from various ingredients was a brilliant experience. It was personal nourishment and made me feel good and brought me joy. Measuring the correct amount of flour or butter and cracking the exact number of eggs, marinating the meat or peeling and preparing vegetables or a fresh salad was like meditation for me. I had to be in the moment, adding ingredients, adjusting the heat of the oven or grill and tasting the food to make sure everything was coming together nicely. That great smell in the kitchen after pulling a freshly-baked loaf or a batch of fruit scones out of the oven and the good feeling that comes with it. I was being creative, it was therapeutic and I was learning a new skill. Remember the numbers of people baking banana bread in the early stages of the COVID19 pandemic went through the roof!

I began reading books for some mental stimulation and to reduce stress. Dolores and I would often head to Howth or Portmarnock for long walks by the sea. I got back cycling and joined a club in nearby Dunboyne, Co. Meath. Dolores was a nurse in the Hermitage Clinic in Lucan doing twelve hour shifts. I'd have the dinner ready when she came home. I started to re-educate and retrain myself. I did many courses and programmes and I started to get work around Dublin in the only industry I knew well, the transport industry. I worked as a Transport Consultant and Driver Trainer. I went on to become a Gold Accredited Driver and acquired a Diploma in Advanced Driving. This opened up more doors for me and I was also qualified to do classroom presentations, driver training and assessments. I worked with the Freight Transport Association FTA – and the CPL Group training and recruitment and other training companies around the Leinster area in particular. My recovery was slow and steady.

Living in Dublin and the anonymity it brought was giving me the space to breathe and exist without the constant pressure and reminders of the turmoil and trauma I had been going through. It wasn't all plain sailing though. I regularly got flashbacks along with feelings of despair and loneliness. I was particularly missing my children and grandchildren and my sister Fionnuala's kids. At times I was filling my head with loads of questions and doubts. Would I ever get fully over this? Was I to blame? How did it go so wrong? How can I move on? I had good days and bad days. A sad song on the radio or a certain type of scene in a film or a TV programme played on my mind and kick started an avalanche of emotions. Walking through a shopping centre and meeting grandparents entertaining grandchildren often upset me. Some days I felt drained from it all, empty and scarred, wounded, deflated and even useless.

Gradually, with the passing of time these days and moments became few and far between. I began to repair and to get some of my spark back and my enthusiasm started to return, my spirits began to lift and I was getting stronger. I was slowly beginning to enjoy my life in Dublin. We had a busy Spar shop on the main Clonsilla Road close to the entrance to our estate and I called in regularly for bits and pieces. I knew the first names of all the employees most of whom were foreign nationals. I knew their kids names and took an interest in their stories. I am a people person always was. I missed the west coast and its spectacular scenery and moody weather, but most of all I missed talking to friendly people who answered you when you bid them the time of day.

After spending a couple of years in Dublin, Dolores got the chance to take early retirement and we made the decision to move to Galway. It was not an easy decision for Dolores as she had two adult children in Dublin. Since leaving her native Kerry and the village of Duagh thirty seven years previously she always said she would like to move back to the countryside and the west coast.

I had brought her to Kinvara one weekend in the middle of winter and she fell in love with the place. Finding a house took time, but we managed to make the move in June 2015. We now live on the Doorus Peninsuala just four kms.outside of Kinvara overlooking the ocean and the Burren. A dream location for someone like myself who is comfortable in the outdoors, for walks, hiking, cycling and sea sports. We settled into the community very quickly and we were accepted as a couple. It was like a new beginning in a new location for both of us. I put a tipper truck on the road again and attempted to get back into that line of business. I worked extremely hard for the first year trying to get off the ground. This time around we were assessing the business with a fine-tooth comb. After twelve months I realised I was making no money and killing myself punching in twelve/fourteen hour days. Dolores and myself agreed to give it another three months and monitor the situation closely. Thirteen weeks later we decided to pull the plug and the truck went up for sale. The game had changed massively in the intervening seven years since I was last involved.

Rates had not improved and rising costs and regulations were impossible to manage. I had also changed my outlook. I was not going to be running a business with all its headaches for the sake of running a business and making no margin never mind a reasonable profit. The truck was sold.

Many business owners I see, continue to try and survive running a business when decisions need to be made quickly and with purpose. Sometimes this involves a change of direction or strategy or some other type of streamlining or may need more major surgery. But a business needs constant monitoring and attention and tweaking. Having a coach or mentor can prove very valuable for a business and help you make progress in your personal and professional life. I wish I had the opportunity to bring a coach on board when I was running my business. I know it would have helped me immeasurably.

Having sold off the truck and wrapped up that business I started to seek employment again and went to work for John Sweeney at Sweeney Oil as a Transport Manager/Consultant. I used to have a big fuel account with Sweeney Oil when I had a lot of trucks and machinery so John and myself knew one another well. He was expanding his oil business and increasing his fleet accordingly. I set to work and got stuck in to managing and improving the transport and oil depots. My hard work was somewhat rewarded eighteen months later in 2019 when we scooped an award at the annual 'Fleet Transport Awards' as Transport Operator of the Year in our category. Running a transport business in this day and age entails enormous amounts of record keeping, adherence to regulation and legislation, service records and compliance. Oil company fleets also carry extra regulatory requirements because of the dangerous cargo they store, move and deliver. While I was enjoying the work as a self-employed consultant I felt the level of responsibility and accountability kept climbing and it was taking up as much time as if I were running my own business. I decided to move on. I had other plans in my head.

Ever since the experience of working with a Life Coach in 2008 and many times since then, I had decided I would like to become a Life Coach myself. I took a few weeks off and enjoyed more cycling and hiking. Dolores booked a week in Majorca and later another week in Scotland for us. The downtime was a tonic and I came home refreshed. I had become more focused on where I wanted to be and what I wanted to do. What about my ego? I had forgotten about that! It was another part of my transition. Shortly after starting my Life Coaching course I heard about a Truck and Van sales position for Renault Trucks with Shaw Commercials in Castlebar Co. Mayo. I met Mick Shaw and he offered me the position. After considering it long and hard I eventually accepted the offer on the understanding that I could finish the course. Having later acquired the qualification and become an Accredited Life Coach I settled into the sales role. I was slowly finding my feet and gradually building up a customer base while also doing some Life Coaching and when the Pandemic hit I also had to face a personal health issue at the same time. During my recovery and in the midst of all the enforced restrictions I decided to leave the sales role with Shaws and devote my time and energy fully to the Life Coaching. I had dipped into the transport industry in different ways at this stage and had come full circle. I had made up my mind and decided to go with my gut feeling and devote my full attention to Life Coaching.

My transition continues...

Chapter 9

I FORGED A NEW LIFE AROUND MY PASSION

Steve Rose, PhD wrote a very interesting piece on passion. So, what does it mean to follow your passion? "Following your passion means exploring areas that spark your interest, developing your skills in a specific area, and using those skills to contribute to something beyond yourself."

In March 2020 I was at home recovering after an angioplasty, heart stenting procedure. My blockages necessitated four stents. A result of the chronic stress I had been subjected to ten years previously. My Cardiologist Prof. Sugrue said I would recover quickly. "Your diet and lifestyle are good and you are fit, you will recover quickly, just stay away from the stress," he informed me. The pandemic had kicked in and life as we knew it was about to change very drastically, more so for some than for others, but affecting everyone to some degree. The country was in lockdown and this made it easier for me to slow down and concentrate on my recovery. After a week I was back walking and two weeks later I was on the mountain bike doing laps of a circuit in Doorus near the house. I managed this important and critical time very well. My mindset and motivation were clear and concise. Like the whole population of the world, I was dealing with the pandemic and it's wide-ranging implications, and I was also coming to terms with the shock of having undergone a stenting procedure. My resilience kicked in. I had been in worse personal situations before and found my way through it. I kept it simple. I looked for a few positive things every day. I exercised each day even during the tightest restrictions. I did not allow myself to get caught up in negative social media or radio and TV. I focused on what I could do and the things I could control. I appreciated where I was and the close friends in my life. The 'normal' thing for most people during times of crisis or change is to panic and get caught up in the circumstances. The enormity, the sadness, the fear, the self-pity causing low mood, insomnia, stress, anxiety, anger, irritability, emotional exhaustion and depression.

Fear of becoming sick or losing loved ones as well as the prospect of financial hardship. All these intense stressors and many more are present and having a toxic effect on the majority of the population. Some groups are more at risk – frontline workers, groups with long-term mental health issues, young people and children, the elderly and those with a disability or in poverty. The invisible psychological impact on society is and will be huge as we try to come to terms with the trauma in the aftermath. Much of the effect it had on people was down to personal circumstances. What was your career or business, your family situation and where you lived also came into play. In this regard I was really lucky to live in the countryside beside the sea. We chose to locate here from Dublin city for those very reasons that kicked in during the lockdown. Proximity to the sea and the mountains of the Burren, the space and tranquil surroundings and the closeness to nature and the room to breathe and enjoy it. The biggest change for me was that I now had to pop three pills every day.

I never had to take tablets for anything whatsoever until now. I was on two blood thinners and a cholesterol tablet daily. A friend of mine referred to them as old man tablets! As my recovery progressed well with a mixture of walking, cycling and kayaking I began to think about Life Coaching and how I might progress and expand. As I have alluded to in chapter seven, while on Mount Everest I felt closer to enlightenment. Tibetan Buddhism emphasises compassion and selflessness in order to reach enlightenment. Operating in the company of Sherpas for a few weeks and witnessing their natural ability to brave the staggering heights, their incredible strength to operate at higher altitudes with less oxygen and the deep roots of their religious beliefs and their willingness to show compassion and selflessness is so inspiring. I lay in my sleeping bag many nights in the lap of my own spirituality. It became clear to me that I wanted to progress and train and become a Life Coach. I signed up for the course and became an Accredited Life Coach in 2019. I was doing some one on one sessions with a few clients and slowly building it up during the end of 2019 and early 2020. I had to adapt to zoom sessions during the lockdown. I liked coaching from an early time in my life. I enjoyed coaching players young and old. I loved seeing improvement, growth and development and passing on my experiences. With Life Coaching I had developed new skills especially around active listening, powerful questioning, direct communication and creating awareness for clients. My main characteristics as a 'people person,' I am patient outgoing and friendly. My best three traits concerning others,

Humility - I don't know everything and I am always open and willing to learn. I believe life is fragile and therefore valuable. Curiosity – I have an open mind, I love to listen and learn and absorb and immerse myself. I have a quest for knowledge, culture, beauty and connecting with others. Trying new things and experiences and seeing and exploring new places and challenges. Empathy - I genuinely care and try to understand the world through other people's eyes and appreciate what others are feeling and experiencing. Humility is how you value yourself.

Curiosity is how you value others. Empathy is how you value the bonds between yourself and others. I firmly believe that humility is the soil of knowledge. Curiosity is the water that helps it grow. Empathy is the sunlight that shows us which way to bend. I spoke to Vivienne Molloy a member of our hiking group and a close friend. Viv is a part time lecturer with the Dublin Institute of Design, she runs her own business as a graphic and web designer and is also proficient at social media with over thirty years' experience. We discussed my journey so far. As a result of facing life and mortality as I have, I want to make a difference in the world. I have gained a Master's degree from the university of life. I have operated at the coalface of business and sport and experienced the highs and lows of it all. I have tasted success and extreme loss and personal adversity. I have learnt how to cope and rebuild and develop my resilience. I am an Accredited Life Coach and I want to make a difference to others from what I have learnt on my journey so far.

"Everything can be taken from a man except one thing, The last of the human freedoms, to choose ones attitude in any given set of circumstances, to choose one's own way" – Viktor Frankl.

Vivienne and I decided to formulate a plan. We put our heads together and in May 2020 we co-founded Mind Over Mountains – with the tag line 'Live your best life'. An initiative that combines coaching, mentoring and the great outdoors. Vivienne set to work on building the profile, and Mind Over Mountains (MOM) began to grow quickly for us on all social media platforms. We created some very exciting material which increased our following as people began to recognise MoM for the messages insights and material we were producing. Next to come onboard was Brendán ó hEaghra from his company – Meas Media. Brendán helped steer MoM with his marketing credentials and expertise. We got very positive feedback and comments on what we were promoting. We did short videos in many locations mostly outdoors, on the side of a mountain, on a bike or in a kayak as well as in the office and on street locations. Covering topics such as mindset- goals setting- being stuck- focus- faith- motivation and so on. We also did the A to Z of Life Coaching, shooting all twenty six letters in different places with an emphasis on fun as well as the message behind each letter. Examples of the A to Z = Words beginning with 'A' – Adorable - Altitude – Attitude – Arsehole - How is your attitude? What is your attitude in dealing with things? Are there arseholes in your life? Are you an arsehole at times? Words beginning with the letter 'M' – Magic – Meditate – Miracle – Motivate – Do you meditate? How motivated are you? Will it take a miracle to get you moving? Just a few examples from the A to Z we created. We started doing some pre-recorded interviews with people from different walks of life with really insightful tales to impart. The likes of Tommy O Hanlon on his ongoing battle with what was initially diagnosed as bowel cancer but had spread to his liver and lungs. He wanted to give a strong message to all, that people were struggling and fighting other life-threatening illnesses as well as Covid 19. Tommy portrayed such a positive and humane approach to his own situation. Sadly, Tommy passed away in October 2021 before we got a chance to do another interview, which we had organised.

"Ar dhéis Dé go raibh a anam dilís".

We interviewed Mary Green of Greene's bar in Kinvara. She spoke elegantly about having to close her pub and remain closed for the first time in its 150 year family history due to the pandemic. Her livelihood had come to an abrupt end and she did not know when she might reopen again. Joe Byrne our local County Councillor on life as a local councillor and the satisfaction he gets from helping people and sorting out their issues. My sister's twelve year old son Eoín Gannon and what he finds important in his life. He did kind of refuse to comment on his famous uncle! Our flagship course "Navigating your Pathway" has been very successful- a critical course and a life changing experience for all participants to date. It took us a couple of months to put it together. After extensive research and a blend of life coaching and my own experience we are very happy with what we have produced and the results and feedback has been very pleasing and positive. We feel the programme is structured in such a way that it will help people look at their lives from a different perspective. Creating awareness and taking a helicopter view of every single element of the participants life, facing up to the changes that need to happen and using the tools and exercises provided by the course to work towards setting new goals and planning how to achieve them while remaining accountable. During your weekly journey while doing this programme you are guided and helped to come up with your own answers and your own plan to change your situation and live your best life. For those who roll up their sleeves and get stuck in, the results are defining.

MoM is also enabling people to reach out and plan to do amazing personal challenges or for team events, through motivation the right mindset and discipline. I have a particular grá for this type of work as I have had much success with sporting teams and leading groups and my own personal adventures and achievements. I have experience of what it takes to be successful and to achieve your goal and live your dream. I firmly believe that in order to be successful your mental health and wellbeing is every bit as important as your physical health. Your goals and values must be aligned. You must be aware of your mindset and be clear and concise on the factors that influence you positively and negatively. This applies in sports, in business and corporate organisations and to all individuals in all walks of life. Society is slowly becoming more receptive to coaching. The pandemic has made us look at our lives from a different perspective. Life has become more challenging, routines and habits have been turned upside down. The familiar has been replaced by the unknown and uncertainty. We are the same humans but the world we live in has changed considerably. Some thrive in these situations, however the majority struggle. Take time and go back into the locker room or the dressing room and re-evaluate and rethink as you prepare to enter this new arena, this different world. You have a chance to make changes to reinvent and to design a better life for yourself.

Do not miss this opportunity to live a more fulfilling existence with more emphasis on your mental and physical health and wellbeing. Whether it's personal or business or sporting. Coaching will always come down to 'life issues'. It's working with people's lives, providing clients with support as they transition through change. As a coach you do not judge your client, you must work with them and move at their pace. By asking powerful questions you help a client tap into their own resources and find their own answers. The results usually work better for people as they have found their own solutions. I have seen and experienced personally the massive benefits of working with a Life Coach. It was a hugely transitional move for me at a time when I was very vulnerable and struggling to find a way forward. I am very adamant that the kick start I required for finding my way and the answers and direction I needed began when I started going to a Life Coach and has continued ever since.

My personal growth journey to becoming a Life Coach has been most rewarding. I now have a more complete understanding of my own life. I am better placed to accept the difficulties I have encountered along the way. I have walked the walk and I am confident that I can talk the talk. I appreciate that it is a big decision for people to make, to reach out and decide to work with a coach. People do not put enough value on personal development or spending money on themselves in this way. I'm sure if you have ever entertained the thought of changing your life some of the blockages that you have come up with look like the following.

It's too expensive to hire a Life Coach: I don't have enough time: I can Coach myself: I can't trust someone else with my issues: I don't need someone to tell me how to live my life: I won't do it right: I will be judged: It won't be confidential: It won't help: My partner will not approve: My brother or sister will not support me: My parents will be affected.

None of the above is true. The benefits once you get started are enormous. You will change your life. You will face the truth and the reality of your life. You will take charge of your own life and take responsibility for it. That is powerful and empowering at the same time. You will take ownership and show up and keep coming back and be accountable. You will design your own solutions and find answers and the power and direction to make the changes you want to make in your life. You will also learn to let go of your ego and face your true self, find self-compassion and self-love. When is the last time you made a decision about your own mental and physical health and wellbeing? During your transition you will learn to let go of what is and what is not and ultimately find peace and contentment and a better more fulfilling life. You learn to become aware and analyse your situation and then you focus on what you can change or control and you take action. Letting go of what is not realistic and out of your control. After this comes the sense of achievement and your commitment going forward. Hop on a free discovery call or a chemistry call and ask some questions and see if you might like to work with a coach, find out if you are both suited to work together. No matter how many bottles of wine you have, or how much weights you lift, or how many chocolates you eat, or how many nice clothes or pairs of shoes you buy, or how many hours or days you work, it won't make these issues you have go away. It's vital to share your troubles, your fears and your triumphs and not try to shoulder it all. You are creating a life with less stress, less worry, less time depressed and under pressure. You will also get rid of limiting beliefs and negative emotions, increase your confidence and your self-esteem.

Many coaches will only work with clients for between three and twelve months and some clients prefer this long-term relationship to help create fundamental change. Clients often go away from the first few sessions buzzing with excitement and full of plans and goals. Then the full force and realisation of what they have taken on dawns on them and they can easily fall off the wagon. I have had some clients who have done exactly that. After a few weeks or months human nature and the initial weaknesses kick into play. The beginning is insightful and clients see the areas where change and improvements are needed. New goals are set and the journey begins. It feels good initially to be making your own decisions and affecting your own changes. However, life has a habit of putting fences in the way and throwing some difficulties at you from time to time. From my own experience this is the critical space if you are to push through and achieve your goals and continue on your path of personal development, or really make the changes that you identified earlier, the improvements you decided you needed to make to your life. But the very reasons you decided to improve your life in the first place are now trying to derail you and throw you off your path. The habits and excuses and not facing up to all areas in your circle of life are coming up. The self-blame, self-critical, negative and judgemental side are making a strong case to be heard. Or you decide to apportion blame onto others or circumstances or conditions. In short – you cop out! Personal change is not easy. It forces you to give up old habits and beliefs and makes you question your core values and jolts you into consciousness sometimes in uncomfortable ways. It also causes ripple effects with others, family, friends, work, career and so on. I have found that when you identify discomfort and dissatisfaction and stress in your life, then you must address that. My question for you as you read through my book is......"What do you want in life?" No ifs or buts or maybes – answer the question for yourself. "What do you want in life?" Look at all areas – business, career, family, relationships, friends, pastimes, health and wellbeing, self-care, finances. What are your priorities? Do you have clear priorities? How are you managing your time? If you have some thoughts about it, write out your answers in your diary or get a journal. Then write down your goals as to how you are going to achieve whatever it is you want in your life.

Develop this exercise further. What are your feelings about what might stop you or is stopping you at this very moment. Anxiety, fears, trauma, past-illness or experiences, self-conflict, self-blame, self-confidence, self-assurance, self-criticism, finances, timing. Maybe its pressure from other significant influences in your life, your parents, brother, sister or partner, or your boss or work colleagues or your friends. Is achieving what you want based around the correct time or having enough money? I urge you to bring health, love, happiness and inner peace into your thoughts and onto your journal along with freedom and kindness and appreciation. Are you focused on the material things in the world or are you looking for more fulfilment and a deeper level of peace and happiness? Who are the people you are spending most of your time with? Have they a positive or negative influence on you? Where are your values and beliefs? Your values and beliefs not anyone else's.

It is becoming very clear to me as we exit the pandemic and it's aftereffects, as society adjusts and attempts to get going again, that everything is being ramped up. For many, greed is taking over and the excessive demand for supremacy, to be the best, to be the biggest, to make the most, to have the most. The new badge of honour, "I'm flat out, we can't keep up with it, we're inundated with orders, I don't have a minute, we're working seven days a week!!" We have been in this territory before during the Celtic Tiger and I was personally caught up in it. The lessons from the past should be a marker for the future. Many people made huge personal adjustments to their lives during the various lock downs. Taking up some form of exercise and recreation, developing their talents through cooking, reading, gardening and DIY. Spending more time with family and loved ones and generally improving their lifestyle and wellbeing. Many have abandoned these changes in some cases completely as their focus has returned to the materialistic side of life. Others have had to readjust to the demands of having to return to work fully in some form.

Adjusting to this 'new normal' is easier said than done. People are exhausted and feel tired, and have no enthusiasm and feel depleted in some cases. Personal and work relationships have been negatively affected. Based on my own experience and dealing with my own trauma and stress a couple of years ago, I believe acceptance is the key. I don't mean giving up. I mean not resisting or fighting reality and wasting valuable energy doing so. You will probably say to yourself, I did not plan or want to be here or have to deal with this. It is tough but that's the way it is. Use your energy to create a more spacious mental space that allows you to start doing things that are constructive instead of being stuck in a state of psychological self-torment. Stop being hard on yourself and give yourself the opportunity to replenish more. Stop looking for and listening to negativity, if this is part of your environment, change it and the people you spend time with. Look for those who are positive and active and fun to be around. In my own case, I found it a period of self-discovery. I started to learn about myself at a deeper level. How is your mood today as you read this chapter? You cannot keep fighting the world every single day. It is not good for your mental health. Make some small changes. Much the same as what I did, you must build your resilience. Focus on exercise, getting out in the fresh air, nutrition, sleep, meditation, self-compassion, gratitude, connection and saying no. Start really small and increase it gradually. Don't over complicate it and try to make big changes all together. Work on one or two things every week and the improvements will kick in as you build momentum and this will improve your mood and mental health. Some days and weeks will be more difficult than others, allow yourself some compassion and be kind and considerate. You will gradually build your own resilience. Stop being closed minded and fixated with your thinking, this will keep you stuck and unable to move forward or work on what you are lacking in your abilities. To improve yourself and grow and become the person you always wanted to become, you must be open to all possibilities of growth. You have the power to change and transform your life once you start evolving. Acknowledge and work through your pain and suffering and the mixed emotions that come with change. By operating with a growth mindset you are open to develop and improve your knowledge and abilities and to learn and develop as a person. Eliminate excuses and put your plan in place and start making adjustments that will help you to transform your life.

"I was always looking outside myself for strength and confidence, but it comes from within. It is there all the time". – Anna Freud, Psychoanalyst.

Acceptance for me in 2008-2009-2010 was really difficult as I struggled mentally with the trauma and loss I was suffering and trying to come to terms with. I wasted piles of energy and tons of stress trying to fix parts of my life. The mountains in my mind were colossal as I shouldered the self-blame for my circumstances. Once I began to accept my situation, my mental washing machine slowed down. On some good days it was on a normal cycle. The stress became less and more bearable. I started managing myself in a more positive manner, dealing with small things that were within my control and being kinder on myself. To a large degree I have successfully continued to do so for the last ten years. I do wobble occasionally and my form can take a dip. This does not happen too often nowadays and if I feel it coming on I organise to have a chat with a close friend. As I mentioned earlier putting my thoughts together for this book caused me a lot of emotional upset in certain chapters more than others. I know how it feels to have to deal with some shit that you would rather leave well behind in the rear view mirror. But our minds and our acceptance or denial of issues and circumstances can play tricks on us. These thoughts and personal moods can be triggered at any time by the simplest of things and we start to slip mentally. Much like a snowball that starts off small and in a short time it becomes huge. The driver in front of you is driving too slow, the lady at the checkout with the screaming child. The guy at work that always comes in late. If you are carrying some stress at this time then any one of these can drive you mad. Keeping your mental health in good shape is a full time job. It takes time and effort and controlling your mindset is a huge part of it. Make room in your daily schedule for yourself.

Slow down and breathe and take the foot off the throttle. In June of 2021 I did some work with Scott Ballard-Life Coach-Author-Confidence Coach-Business Coach- Guest Speaker. Scott is based in Portland, Oregon USA. During our work together Scott skilfully guided me from my youth right through my life up to where I am today. I have been coached many times over the last twelve years but Scott and myself went to a much deeper level this time. I was ready willing and able to do some deep work. His powerful probing questions had me searching deep within for answers. Often it took me a couple of minutes before I could respond. During some sessions he asked me "Why was I living a lie?" Or he would make reference to "You are living a lie". I took great offence to his question and suggestion. I became agitated and disagreed with him and said I was truthful and honest with my words and actions. He made me realise that while I had accepted what had happened in my life especially around losing my businesses and the ending of my marriage and the fallout that ensued. "You have spent the last twelve or thirteen years accepting the blame for all of that. It was not all your fault. You have climbed in under a rock and you are still carrying it around with you. You are stuck at base camp". He continued, " You were caught up in a global financial crisis and your businesses became casualties, some marriages do end and it's never one person's fault. You have been very successful in your life, in business and sport and your adventures from a very early age and you now have a massive opportunity to help others with your chosen career, get out and away from base camp and you will lead many others to summit their own mountains". He then asked me to write a letter of apology to myself in the form of an email and send it to himself. It took me over two and a half hours to write that letter. I apologised to myself in great detail about occasions and events that have transpired in my sixty years. I forgave myself for accepting total responsibility for many situations and circumstances that were out of my control. I apologised for holding myself as a prisoner and for losing my voice and my identity in my own life. I forgave myself for having bottled up my feelings and opinions and the right to express myself. In my letter I released myself from living a lie! I also acknowledged my successes and my strength of character and resolve, my tremendous empathy and understanding of others. I committed to move away from base camp and to lead many others away from their personal struggles. My own struggles will become my success story. The combination of writing that letter and the powerful deep level work Scott and myself did over a couple of weeks was hugely transformational. I feel that my effectiveness, performance, personal development and growth increased measurably. I have walked away from two good career positions in the last four years. Many would say I jumped off a cliff with no parachute. I do not agree. I see too many people stay stuck in ill-fitting careers for a sense of security, certainty and confidence and never make a change. I could not ignore my own deepest impulses.

I could no longer live someone else's idea of a wonderful life. I am passionate about what I am now doing. Setting up Mind Over Mountains with Vivienne has given me an opportunity to use my experience and abilities to help others, to make a difference in the world. I had the luxury of being able to choose a career that I am passionate about and I have done so. It will take time before MoM is financially viable but I believe that will happen as we watch its gradual growth unfold. There is nothing more satisfying than working with clients and see them develop, find their own strengths and confidence and improve their lives. My own personal journey continues and I find this hugely exciting. I am learning more about myself and people in general every day. My education and research is more a part of my everyday life than ever before. I have just signed up for my next programme. The ability to regulate mood, to stay positive and resilient, to be able to handle ups and downs, remain even keeled and to deal with unpredictable misfortune without losing your grip. In my early years I believed that temperament was fixed. A person is either weak (tends to choke under pressure) or strong (tend to come through). I have definitely changed my thinking on this based solely on my own experiences in life, sport and adventures. I have been invited to do the programme based on my pedigree. The mental state you want to avoid and the one you want to be in. The All-Blacks call it Red Head/Blue Head as I have referenced in Chapter Six.

Although the All-Blacks are the most well-known users of the concept, largely because of the high profile results they have achieved, it's actually a training method also used by teams and individuals all over the world. The red to blue mental skills concept has been developed and perfected and can be adapted and tailored to suit any situation. The ability to think clearly and remain mentally on task is huge especially under pressure. I'm excited to participate in this programme and have it as part of my arsenal of offerings for my clients going forward. I have developed my own understanding of my own personal triggers and responses to stay in the Blue under pressure. Having set up my own mechanisms over the years and having had to use them many times, as a result I do react well under pressure and I am eager to learn more during this programme. More learnings and more growth and attaining more knowledge and information to be able to share with others. Exciting times ahead for Mind Over Mountains.

Wrap up - September 07 - 2021 – Tuesday Morning

I left the house in Kinvara at 6.45am this morning heading for Connemara. I am now standing in the same location in Indreabhán I mentioned in Chapter Five earlier in this book. The place where I contemplated ending it all twelve years ago. I feel strange, reluctant almost to be here. As I walk along the shore and on to the rocky coastline and retrace my steps to where I stop with the ocean below me. Memories come flooding back as I remember the cold, wet, windy mornings I used to experience at this very location. I am reminded of the thoughts and turmoil and feelings of helplessness and embarrassment I experienced at that time. The hairs are standing on the back of my neck. I feel a slight sweat on my brow. My heart is beating a bit faster. A strange nervousness has engulfed me since I got out of the car. A part of me does not want to be here. Another part of me knows that this is something I must do. I am now standing at what was my dark place on many mornings in the toughest of times. My mind fills up like a jungle of thoughts, flashbacks to those horrible mornings of never-ending stressful emotions and feelings. My eyes begin to well up and I can't control the small tear drops that slide down both sides of my face. It hurts deep inside me once again. If you have experienced this type of feeling you will identify with what I am saying.

Today is different. The sun is coming out and there is a lovely soft refreshing breeze hitting my face coming in off the Atlantic. I briefly close my eyes and take a deep breath and smell the sea and allow it to calm me down. I listen to the beautiful sound of the ocean and it suddenly feels ok. So much has changed since the last time I was here. I'm wearing a pair of shorts and a round neck t-shirt, light hiking shoes and sunglasses. I am leaner and in much better shape and feeling fit and strong. My t-shirt should carry a slogan – "survived a few wars – took a few hits - picked up a few injuries – learned to cope and adapt and rebuild - and here I am". Outside of my good physical health, I have also addressed my mental health and wellbeing. Some baggage still remains and some of the results of my wars are very real and painful. I still deal with some of those consequences every single day of my life. The blood flow through my arteries to my heart is aided by four stents and I somehow manage standing, walking, running, cycling and mountaineering with a gammy knee. The mental and emotional side of dealing with certain elements is the most painful. It never goes away.

Today, at this moment, I feel calm and content. I don't blame myself now. I am not totally responsible. The weight has lifted. I have moved on. My growth and personal development continues. Our mental health and wellbeing are where I believe our true balance is found. However, creating health – orientated habits rather than illness - oriented services is more difficult and where many struggle. The World Health Organisation (WHO) declares that health is "A state of complete physical, mental and social wellbeing and not merely the absence of disease or infirmity". Based on my own experiences I now more than ever strongly believe that as individuals we must promote wellbeing rather than treating illness. Our wellbeing needs to become the norm rather than the exception for our mental health. We all have to realise that we possess the ability to cope with the normal stresses of life, we can work productively and fruitfully, and we can make a contribution to our communities. My recovery and transformation have taken time and will always carry a 'work in progress' slogan. We are all the same in that regard. For those who decide to make changes and take control and start to live your best life, the journey is ongoing but very rewarding. Wrapped up in the same process you need to develop acceptance and a willingness to change is pivotal. Facing up to yourself, your true core, your true being is incredibly difficult. It's convenient to blame others or your circumstances. We tend to focus on only one or two areas in our lives and park and ignore the other more personal stuff. As a result, we carry the stress that normally accompanies that decision for many years. If you're struggling with your health and wellbeing, your habits and methods and environment are no doubt contributing to your problems. That way of life I would describe as existing, not living. Be brave, ground yourself, stand up on your own two feet and address the areas that need to change in every part of your life. No excuses or kicking the ball down the road. Become a more fulfilled individual and renew your personality and lifestyle. You can do it. Stop living a lie! I reached out for help. I set realistic goals and dealt with one task at a time. I eventually got comfortable in my own skin and slowly rebuilt my confidence. I nurtured some relationships and connected with others. I became active and ate well. I took time out for things I enjoyed (even the really simple things). I learned to manage stress and improve sleep and get more rest. I built my resilience during this process. I live a very colourful life. I fill it with adventures and activities and fun. Vivienne and I set up Mind Over Mountains with a lifestyle theme and 'Live your best Life' tag line. We love promoting this brand. My career is now about helping others find the strength and courage to step up and become whatever it is they want to become. Through managing mindset and motivation and promoting personal growth.

Every single one of us is on a different journey. Every single day we endeavour with our minds to help us get over our personal mountains. From reading this book and spending some time with me on my journey, I hope you will appreciate and understand the good and the not so good in your own life. I have had many fabulous adventures and remarkable achievements. I have a few very important people in my life. I have real friends that I can count on one hand. I terribly miss certain others and pray that someday that will change. I have overcome adversity in many forms that life has thrown in my direction. Many of my mountains have been steep and hard. I believe I have become more complete, understanding and empathetic as a result. My struggles have taught me many lessons and developed my emotional intelligence and humility. My message to you is not based on what I was taught by any organisation or acquired in any college or institution. I have chosen to bare my soul to you, to be vulnerable and naked about my inner thoughts and deepest feelings. I have really struggled with some chapters. Bleeding on my typewriter has regurgitated the good,the bad and the ugly and highlights the alarming depths I had slipped too. It has also been therapeutic and monumental in my personal growth. I hope you enjoy the good, appreciate the bad and learn from the ugly.

Slán tamall.

"Is fear an tsláinte ná na táinte" - *"Health is better than wealth".*

About The Author

A Connemara man, Máirtín Óg grew up in the West of Ireland in the Gaeltacht village of Carraroe, county Galway. His father died when Máirtín Óg was only eight years old which had a profound impact on his later life. An injury in his early 20s forced an abrupt end to a promising football career. Máirtín Óg built a multimillion euro plant and machinery business only to lose it all in the economic collapse of the Celtic Tiger. Thus, he has seen his fair share of 'ups' and 'downs' from the highs of cycling 3000 miles across America, climbing to base camp of Mount Everest with his son to the lows of financial ruin, family breakdown and contemplating ending it all. Máirtín Óg takes us through some of his action-packed and incident-filled life journey weaving within it his eternal optimism, infectious enthusiasm, warm Connemara charm and the lessons he hopes to pass on to those who might have stopped believing they can fulfil their dreams.

Máirtín Óg now lives in Kinvara, South Galway with his partner Dolores and Ruby the cat. An active hiking leader, he is often seen on the hills and mountains of the Burren and Connemara with his groups or cycling around Ireland's beautiful coastline with his buddy, Sean Kelly.

Using his vast life experience with all its highs and lows Máirtín set up Mind Over Mountains to help individuals and groups navigate their own pathways through life, focusing on nurturing a positive mindset, prioritising and achieving clarity in all areas of their lives. The central message of this book is that each of us can find happiness within, beyond the material things in life, if we choose to look deep into our minds and hearts.

Vivienne Molloy, Co Founder and Brand Consultant of Mind Over Mountains
Máirtín Óg Mc Donagh, Life Coach and Co Founder of Mind Over Mountains